Faces and Places
Of
Yesterday

Loretta Merrell Ekis

Overland Park, KS   Published 2014

i

Faces and Places of Yesterday

The J. E. Parker peddling truck pictured on the preceding page was driven by different drivers. Two men that are well-remembered as drivers were John Whitt and T. L. Ferguson. This picture was made in the 1940's during what appears to be a heavy snowfall. The truck was connected to J. E. Parker Grocery in Cash Point. Robert Laten and John Whitt each were operators and owners of the store at some time in the 1940s to 1950s. Joe Roper owned the store throughout much of the 1950's and until he had to retire a few years ago.

The peddling trucks were common in the area during the 1940s and possibly into the early 1950s. They carried a wide variety of goods, and were simply a traveling store. Ladies and men in the community would meet the truck when it stopped in front of their homes and purchase needed items such as flour, cornmeal, sugar, and other things. Children were always excited to see the truck because they also carried sweets for purchase. If not for the peddling trucks, farm women would have had to travel to the store in Cash Point or Ardmore to obtain some of the necessities of life, and many farm wives of that day did not drive or have access to an automobile.

One bonus for the ladies is that the flour sacks came in printed fabrics that could be used to make aprons, dishtowels and even dresses if the lady of the house was fortunate enough to get two or more of the same design. Bags of flour were large so the bags provided lots of fabric. Many a depression/war era child sported flower sack dresses and underwear.

These trucks were always welcomed and swarmed by children at almost every stop. To say they were popular would not be an understatement. Everyone loved the Peddling Truck and its driver.

"Each photograph is a story captured in a single moment"

M.Lopez

Faces and Places of Yesterday

Title:	Faces and Places of Yesterday
Author:	Loretta Merrell Ekis
Published by:	Loretta Merrell Ekis 7204 West 155th Street Overland Park, KS
Date:	August 2014, Revised September 2014
ISBN	ISBN-13: 978-1500790950

Available from Amazon.com, CreateSpace.com, and other retail outlets

Dedication

This book is dedicated to the memory of all who were involved in shaping the communities of Cash Point, Ardmore and the surrounding area.

Acknowledgement

I began this book as one of photos only, and it was well on its way to completion (at least 80 pages of it was) when the computer decided I didn't need the copy any longer and mysteriously deleted the entire book from my files. After searching for a week, using everything at my disposal to locate the deleted file, I finally decided to start over and expand the book to include more history.

To that end I owe a multitude of thanks to several people who have furnished photos and historical information for this book. First, Peggy Hargrave Holt who tirelessly gathered and scanned many pictures, as did Anna Smith Massey. Also, thanks to Faye and Bill Hand who helped me with information and photos, Verlin Collins for getting approval for use of some of the photos, and Beverly Browning, Robbie Hayes, Laurene Schrimisher and others. Kenneth Smith has provided me access to some photos and much of his research about Cash Point and the surrounding area. Without his help, a lot would be missing from this book. I am forever grateful for all contributions. Also, I want to thank Your Community Shopper: Joe Stagner, Patti Stagner, Patricia Coulter and Linda Keith for their help in advertising the book and helping with distribution when needed.

Writers typically have to work alone. It is the nature of our work, but because of this we are indebted to our support system—people who help us and want us to succeed. So a huge thanks to all who have aided in the writing of this book. It is your history, and I hope that it will bring you much pleasure in the days and weeks to come.

Disclaimer

In writing this book, it was my decision to include stories of the community—some that were good, some that were bad and some that were ugly. All the information I've included in this book has been public for many years in various publications. However, if I have offended anyone, I offer my sincere apologies. My belief is that history is history and rewriting it is not a choice.

About the Author

Loretta Merrell Ekis grew up in the Ardmore-Cash Point area along with her six siblings. She was a member of Cash Point Baptist Church for many years and attended school at Cash Point, Ardmore and Blanche where she graduated in 1956.

The author has a deep interest in the history of the community and a desire to preserve it along with photos of many who have already passed on to eternal rest. Genealogy has been a great interest of hers for many years, and she has published or co-published three books:

1. A History of the Tennessee Branch of the Merrell Family Of Tennessee - co-authored by Marie Merrell Broadway and Faye Merrell Hand, published about 1976.

2. Southern Days and Southern Ways, 2013

3. The Blood of Patriots – The Story of Capt. Benjamin Merrell – American Patriot, 2014

Faces and Places of Yesterday

Table of Contents

List of Photos

Faces and Places of Yesterday

Faces and Places of Yesterday

Faces and Places of Yesterday

Faces and Places of Yesterday

Faces and Places of Yesterday

Introduction

During my youth, I often heard the older people in the community say the SW corner of Lincoln County and the SE corner of Giles County were a no-man's land when it came to being noticed by people who ran the counties. In fact, about the only time we saw or heard from the powers that be in either county was a few weeks before election time when the office holders and those seeking office would venture into our small communities to garner votes.

Because of this lack of attention, little has been written in the official county histories about the people who settled in this area which includes Ardmore, Cash Point, Blanche, Kelly's Creek, Union Hill and a portion of Giles County that lies east of I-65 including Bee Springs. That is the reason, I've chosen to focus on this area to preserve old photos and draw attention to a small piece of its history.

This is by no means a complete history of the area. It is simply a "snapshot" of things I and others have gleaned while researching our families. I'm certain there is much, much more history I could include, but that might require a number of years to put it on paper, and frankly, at my age, that might not happen.

I do apologize for the quality of some of the photographs, but many are simple snapshots, faded with time, that were provided me, and I felt they were important to the history of the community. I hope you do, too. Too many times, when the older generation dies, photos that are unlabeled get tossed simply because no one knows who they were. So, this book is designed to help preserve some of those that might disappear into the netherworld of old photographs.

With that being said, I hope that you will grab a glass of good Southern sweet tea, put on your most comfy clothes and fuzzy slippers, and sit back in your easy chair and not only look at the photos included, but enjoy the stories.

Loretta Merrell Ekis
2014

**Old Abandoned Car on the Isaac Gatlin Place off
Stateline Road taken a few years ago** (photo by author)

A Brief History of Lincoln and Giles County

L incoln County Tennessee was established on November 14, 1809 by an act of the General Assembly from a portion of Bedford County.[1] The county was named for General Benjamin Lincoln, a Revolutionary war officer. The legislature also established and funded the purchase of land for a county seat to be called Fayetteville. One hundred acres was purchased from Ezekiel Norris for $100 for the courthouse and town. County seats typically were placed so that anyone within a day's travel could conduct business with the county. Naturally, that travel then was by horse or horse drawn conveyances.

It is impossible to name all the early settlers who came to the county after the Cherokees ceded the land to the U.S. in 1806, but many did come. They came from North Carolina, which at one time extended all the way to the Tennessee River, from South Carolina, Virginia and other points to the east.

These were hardy people who came to the Tennessee Valley to establish homes, communities, and churches. Some of the communities shown on the map of Lincoln County surrounding Cash Point (aka Whitesburg) are: Philpot, Blanche (aka Pleasant Plain), Kelly's Creek, Dellrose, Coldwater, Yukon, Mary's Grove, Taft, McBurg, Cyruston, Kirkland, Skinem, U-Take-It, Macedonia, and more.

Many people, who grew up in the area over the past 50 years, may never have known Skinem by any other name or Kirkland a few miles to the southwest of Skinem. Skinem was originally named McAllister[2]. There are two stories associated with the naming of Skinem. The first is that William Houston McAllister, the first settler who came from South Carolina, was a wagon, buggy and chair manufacturer. He first located at Towry, TN, at the corner of Huntsville Highway and Pleasant Grove Road. His son later moved the factory. McAllister descendants probably still reside in the area because McAllister's attended Blanche School and other schools in the area.

---

[1] Lincoln County Tennessee Homecoming '86
[2] Lincoln County Heritage Book and S McAllister, a descendant

Faces and Places of Yesterday

One story, by a great-great-great-great grandson of McAllister, states that McAllister was a hard core gambler who got into a heated poker game. He bet the town name and lost. The town was then referred to as "Skinem" because he was "skinned" in the game.[3]

Another writer gives the following information on the name. This writer states, Skinem was named for someone who owned a store at the crossroads. There were two stories told at the time. One was that the owner was said to be so mean that if you got cross-ways of him, "he'd skin you." The other story was that he was such a sharp merchant, "he'd skin you." [4]

So take your pick, and while you're selecting the story, here's another interesting tidbit: Kirkland was originally named Oak Grove because of all the large oak trees that grew there. The Oak Grove community was also known as Frogville—apparently because of the swamp land east and south of the small town. Dele Moncalm McMillan is said to have given it that name.

In the 1940's Pauline Towry felt the town should have a more dignified name and the state granted permission for the name change. Even if there is still some swampy land nearby, the name Kirkland seems far more fitting for this community of neat homes and a lovely church, or kirk, the latter of which is Scottish for church.

Another little community that no longer exists was called Tricky. It was located near the Kelly's Creek Community but closer to New Grove Baptist Church. It was named for James Franklin "Trickey Jim" Smith who owned a store in the area.

Stories about "Trickey Jim" were often told around the old coal stove and fireplace years ago, but most were probably embellished or perhaps not embellished enough, depending on the storyteller. Unfortunately, the little community of Tricky has been mostly forgotten, and few who are now living have heard of it.

Cash Point also had a name change. It started off as Whitesburg, but was changed to its current name. Other interesting place names in the Area are U-Take-It, Po'Grab, Kelly's Creek, Harms and Pleasant Plains.

---

[3] www,city-data-com/forum/Tennessee towns and names

Faces and Places of Yesterday

Giles County was a dense cane-brake when early settlers came to the area. Indians were living in close proximity to the settlers, and they often passed through to their hunting grounds. Sometimes they came to plunder and steal. Thus early settlers not only had to brave the elements, clear land, establish farms and homes, and plant crops, but constantly stay on the alert for marauders. The county was named for William Branch Giles of Virginia, a congressman who aided in Tennessee's admission into the Union in 1796.

Giles County was formed in 1810 by an act of the Tennessee General Assembly. It was formed out of Maury County and has an area of 600 square miles. [5] Before the county was chartered, the area was part of the state of North Carolina.

The first white persons who came to Giles County appear to be those involved in laying out the district. It is believed that the first permanent settlement was made on the Elk River near what is now Prospect.

The first settlers included Absalum Tatum, Isaac Shelby, Anthony Bledsoe, William Bradshaw and James and Elijah Robertson. The early settlers came to Giles County by two routes: by water coming down the Tennessee and up to the Elk River to Richland Creek, and over land coming by way of the Cumberland Gap and Kentucky. Elkton and Prospect clam the distinction of being settled first. Other communities such as Lynn Creek, Campbellsville, Pulaski, Bodenham, Cross Water, Blooming Grove and Aspen Hill came into being soon after Elkton and Prospect. Pulaski was formed and named as county seat due to its central location in the county. The name Pulaski comes from Count Casimir Pulaski, who fell in the attack on Savannah in 1779.

The first county commissioners were James Ross, Nathaniel Moody, Tyree Rodes, Gabriel Bumpass and Thomas Whitson. They were selected primarily due to where they lived so as to represent the entire county.

---

[5] A Brief Sketch of The Settlement and Early History of Giles County by James McCallum, 1876.

Faces and Places of Yesterday

The first magistrates for Giles County were John Dickey, Jacob Baylor, Somerset Moore, Charles Neely, Robert Stelle, Nathaniel Moody, William Phillips, Benjamin Long, Thomas Westmoreland, David Porter and Maxmillian Buchanan. Thomas Steward was named Judge of the 4th District and Alfred Balch was named Attorney General.

The City of Elkton was established in 1886, and had a population of between 150 and 200 people.[6] There were two towns established in the beginning. One was immediately at the mouth of Richland Creek and the other just a short distance below that. They were named Upper and Lower Elkton, which no doubt was somewhat confusing to any newcomer in the area.

Sometime later, another town was laid off about three miles above the upper town on Elk River. Here lots were sold by Dr. Purcell and some others. This town was also named Elkton, but without any adjective added to the name such as was the case of Lower and Upper Elkton. Within a few years, Lower and Upper Elkton lost their identities with citizens moving from there--sometimes into Elkton. The City of Elkton, the third village established in the end became the only Elkton in the vicinity.

Businesses at Elkton in the late 1880s included two general merchandise stores owned by A. W. Moore and T. E. Dailey. A. G. Ezell and Milton Carter, J. J. Upshot, John R. Beasley and P. W. Nave all had dry goods and grocery stores. Two blacksmiths who operated in Elkton were N. M. Hollis and Company and Stephen Dunn. There were two White Churches and one Black Church in Elkton at that time. The Methodist Episcopal and Cumberland Presbyterian served the White population and the Colored Missionary Baptist Church served the Black population.

According to Goodspeed's history of Giles County, there was one chartered high school or academy that served the town along with a common school for the Blacks.

While names found among the writings in Giles County include those who settled as near as Elkton, there were numerous other settlers

---

[6] Goodspeed's History of Giles County, TN 1886

who came into Giles County and settled across the river closer to Ardmore. These settlers who came in the early 1800's, include: Calverts, Majors, Merrells, Morrell's, Hamiltons, Sherrells, Pattersons, Smiths, Thompsons, Lewters and many more. Ardmore came into being about 1910 when the railroad was built from Decatur to Nashville and Alex Austin established a general merchandise store there.

L&N Railroad Construction about 1910-11 near Ardmore in Giles County, Tennessee

Old Cash Point School – about 1920 in Lincoln County, TN. Picture was made from the Currin home which later became the Baptist parsonage.

Faces and Places of Yesterday

Photo of Ardmore Depot made early 1970's.

First Ardmore School on the Tennessee side (photo courtesy Eugenia Curtis)

Early Settlers in the Cash Point Area

T hose who first settled in the Cash Point area were mostly farmers, but there were some businesses established in the small community before the turn of the 20th century. Cash Point was originally named Whitesburg for the Whites who first settled there. It is located on Highway 110 where Asa Smith Road and Minnie Brown Road meet about three miles northeast of Ardmore.

A post office was established in Cash Point in 1877.[7] In order to serve the community, Mrs. Tennie Bledsoe rode a few miles to the east to Pleasant Plains (Blanche) and collected the mail. Her trip was made on horseback apparently in all kinds of weather. Mrs. Bledsoe later operated the Greyhound Bus Station in Ardmore. In later years, the Cash Point post office was closed and mail came out of Ardmore. Ardmore Post Office continues to serve the community to this day.

John Gatlin was one of the earliest settlers, perhaps along with Abijah White, a forefather of the White family that eventually settled in Ardmore. Gatlin was said to be a very energetic man who could "move mountains." It is known that he made and sold wine, apparently legally, to make a living. [8] Another Gatlin, who is believed to have been closely related to him and settled just south of Cash Point was Isaac Gatlin. Isaac had a government still on his land. It was one of many the government contracted to make alcohol prior to the Civil War. Years later, a descendant of John Gatlin, A.D. Gatlin, had a store in which he sold fertilizer just west of the center of Cash Point on Highway 110 in the 1940's and '50's.

Abijah White owned a store on his farm, and moved it to where Asa Smith Road stops at Highway 110. It is said that he placed a name on his store that said Cash Point. One elderly resident who is now deceased said that he was quoted as saying, "You'd pay cash for a pint, so why not name it Cash Point." Probably pronounced as Cash Pint, but there is no proof of that. Another said, White offered goods for "Cash on the Point."

Another settler was T. M. White, descendant of Abijah, who owned a store and a gin at Cash Point. Mr. Tommy White later moved to

---

[7] Lincoln County Homecoming 86
[8] Lincoln County Homecoming 86

Ardmore and set up business there. The old White building, a two story brick building built near the old depot, still stands. Mr. White also started Ardmore Telephone Company in the 1920s, and it was owned by him and later his son, Haney White, until 1948 when it was sold to Fountain Clay Merrell. Merrell who operated the company for over a decade, turned it into a modern dial system and formed a corporation with himself as the first President. The company, under different ownership, continues to serve residents in this area.

Some other families who were early residents in the area were Leatherwood, Philpot, Merrell, Whitt, Ferguson, Roper, Jones, Smith, Gatlin, Barnett, Elliot, Hamilton, Bledsoe, Baird, Darnell, Wallace, Brown, Franklin and more.[9]

Cash Point Baptist Church was organized in 1896. Brush Arbor meetings had been held by Rev. A. C. Smith until a one-room building was built for those meetings.

Official records show that Cash Point Baptist Church was organized March 28, 1896. A council formed of pastors of surrounding Baptist churches met at the school house at Cash Point to advise and assist in the organization of the church.

Those who attended the meeting and presented themselves to the council as members included: Cynthia A. Smith, Mary J. Whitt, Martha J. Wallace, Lula M. White, Francis E. White, Willie F. Whitt, Charlotta F. White, Lena E. White, Clarence Gatlin, Luella J. Whitt, J. B. Whitt, F. R. Wallace, C. B. Whitt, Wiley W. White, N. L. Allsup, D. C. Smith, J. A. Smith, N. S. Smith, Ira A. White, L. P. Johnson, Fannie Johnson, Bobbie Gatlin, T. M. White, all from Piney Grove Church; Martha D. Van Hoozier, W. A. Van Hoozier and N. L. Gatlin of Union Hill Church and J. A. Jones of Kelly's Creek, which made a total of 27 charter members. [10]

The new church then elected Ira A. White, clerk and J. B. White, treasurer. The deacons were F. R. Wallace and N. S. Smith.

The new church was then given the name of Cash Point Missionary Baptist Church. The program of the day shows Rev. W. J.

---

[9] Lincoln County Homecoming '86
[10] Copy of the moderator's notes, M. M. Buchanan

Steward preached on "The Church of God" for the Saturday morning service. On Sunday Rev. Bucker presented the sermon for the 11 a.m. service and Rev. A. R. Smith preached at the 7 p.m. service.

Some changes have been made in the Church since it began as a one room building. The original building was bricked during the community improvement program in the late 1940s, Sunday school rooms and windows were added, and the interior was refurbished at the same time.[11]

The Rev. Raymond Kennedy came to Cash Point Baptist Church in 1948 and served the congregation until 1955 when he moved to Flint River Baptist Church in Madison County, AL. There have been a number of other pastors through the years. Some of these were: Ralph Halbrooks, Elmon Brown, Bert Murphree, William Webb, Glen Hester, David Tipton, William Suddarth, Clarence Stewart, Michael Johnson, David Neal, Larry Bottom, and Derrick Moose, the current pastor.

Cash Point Baptist Church, a one room building, was erected shortly after land owned by Mr. and Mrs. F. R. Wallace was deeded to the church in 1896.

Note that on either side of the one room building classrooms were later added. Heating was originally done with a pot belly stove and lit by gas lights hung from the ceiling. These were acetylene gas lights, combined by

[11] Cash Point Community News, November 1, 1952

mixing calcium carbide and water. Gas was mixed in a small building out back and piped into the church. Electricity was installed in the late 1930s.[12]

Cash Point Baptist Church after 1948 – after it was modernized with brick, windows and more classrooms. This was a typical Sunday morning.

"Precious memories, unseen angels,

Sent from somewhere to my soul;

How they linger, ever near me,

And the sacred past unfold."

---

[12] History of Cash Point Baptist Church, June 1984

Faces and Places of Yesterday

Cash Point Baptist Church as it appears today. It was built beside the original bricked church which is now used for offices, classrooms and other things. In addition a new Family Life Center, not seen in the photo, has been added to provide space for dinners, showers, youth activities and other church events.

Rev. R. B. and Nellie Kennedy
(courtesy of Anna Smith Massey)

11

Asa T. and Jenny Smith Merrell

George Willis (Bitts) Hamilton

Ed and Minnie Barnett

Will and Mary Baird and children Effie and Bessie (Photo courtesy of Kenneth Smith)

Madden and Koy Smith parents of Floyd, Asa, Lorene, Leonard and Leo Smith. Koy was the daughter of Susan Merrell Smith and William Smith.

Andrew and Jennie Stevenson Merrell with son Nathan "Red" Merrell

The Lee Rodgers Family- (Lee, Maggie with Anniece and A.L.)

Oscar and Coy Barnett

Daisy Hargrave, Allene Roper's Mother

Allen Hargrave, 1924, Allene Roper's father

17

James S. Merrell and wife Louisa Josephine Reed Merrell

George W. Merrell and wife Martha C.A. Reed Merrell with son, Andrew

Isaac Thomas Gatlin, 1860's, son of Isaac Gatlin

| **Mary Lou Hamilton Franklin** | **Trudy Hamilton Biles** |

Mary Lou Hamilton Franklin was one of the driving forces in the Cash Point Community improvement years, and due to her untiring efforts much was accomplished. She also served as pianist/organist for the church, and worked diligently to get others involved in the contest and improvements. Mary Lou and Trudy were first cousins. Trudy's family moved to Texas where the family lived through the years. Trudy was the daughter of George "Bitts" Hamilton.

19

This tombstone is located at the Merrell Cemetery on land that George and Cynthia (Syntha) McRee Reed owned, and was later the home of J. S. Merrell. The farm is located on McLemore Road and Kelly's Creek Road. The Reeds along with J.S. Merrell and his wife are buried here. It is a private owned cemetery that was deeded to the eldest daughter of George Reed then to the eldest daughters in that line on down the line to present day. A copy of that deed should still be on file in Fayetteville. The John Willie Lewter family lived in the old home built nearby the cemetery for many years.

'We Caught a Vision'

In the Cash Point Community, things progressed through the late 1800s and into the 1940s with the population increasing about the same as other small communities in the county. There were many hardships experienced during the Civil War, the Great Depression and the years following. County records probably show just how difficult it was for farmers to keep and maintain their homes, and to feed, clothe and educate their children since it was challenging to find work off the farm. The area was referred to as Pea Ridge, which came from the fact that the land was so poor it would only grow peas. After the depression years, growth was slow, crop production was difficult and modernizing homes and businesses was out of the question. The farmland was level, but it was low in minerals. Lots of acres were considered wasteland since it was low and wet ground. Those acres were filled with scrubby bushes and sedge grass. [13]

The WWII years also put a damper on farming in the area due to rationing because of the war effort. By the late 1940s, the name Pea Ridge was still a somewhat derogatory moniker placed on the area, but it was on its way out. But before that happened, much work needed to be done.

In Cash Point, very few homes were painted or had electricity, bathrooms or modern kitchens. Outbuildings were often dilapidated, and mailboxes were rusted and often barely attached to the posts. Fence rows were overgrown, which led one writer to say "(They) were so high that anyone passing the road couldn't see what was growing on the land. In fact, we didn't want others to see our crops, the land produced so little."

The local church was a frame building that had been built almost 50 years before and had seen little improvement. The school building had not had a coat of paint in so long no one could remember

Prior to 1935 no one living in Lincoln County, outside of Fayetteville, had electricity. Even city residents had limited electricity in the 1880s and early 1900s.[14] But the rest of the county lagged much further behind the city.

---

[13] Cash Point Community News, Nov. 1, 1952
[14] Fayetteville Electric, "75 Years of Lighting the Way"

Faces and Places of Yesterday

Those who had the money to operate an in-home generator could have enough electricity to run a few light bulbs at night, but very few people could afford the cost. Instead, much of the county was in the dark and had to use kerosene lamps and candles to aid in their daily chores after sundown.

It wasn't until 1933 when the Tennessee Valley Authority Act was signed that improvements were seen in the valley. These included improved flood control, soil conservation, reforestation, elimination of marginal lands from agricultural use and increased industry.[15] As did the entire valley, Cash Point benefitted from this new authority, as well as the bill that allowed non-profit organizations to borrow money from the government to build rural electric lines. One of those loans came to Lincoln County. As an old song goes, "it was just the start of something big."

There were 53 homes in the Cash Point community in the late 1940's and together they were selling only $1,000 worth of milk a year. Cotton, the main cash crop, produced only 200 to 250 pounds per acre.[16] It was obvious that something had to be done to revive the farms and community.

There were three test farms in the area, and these farms had been operating since 1935. Interested parties in the community toured these farms. They wanted to see if terracing, proper fertilizer application and cover crops made a difference.

While some of the farmers began to see results from new methods and applications, it was really the Community Improvement Contest in 1946 that made Cash Point's development a special event.

The contest was sponsored by the Nashville Chamber of Commerce and communities throughout Middle Tennessee were invited to compete. Ray Ward, assistant agent for Lincoln County, sparked the resident's enthusiasm for the contest. It was because of Ward's zeal that the group was able to "catch a vision."

[15] Fayetteville Electric, "75 years of Lighting the Way"
[16] Looking Backward Through The Years, Cash Point Community News

Ward must have painted a completely renewed community from improved crops to improved homes, church and school when he met with the farmers that evening, because the interest began to build, and the residents were off and running.

The group met the first Thursday night of each month to discuss the needed improvements, and guest speakers were brought in to talk to them about things such as terracing, fertilizers and new methods of farming. Among the leaders then was Grover Owen who often conducted the meetings.

Soon a terracing program was started and farmers added lime and phosphate to their acres. Time and proper weather conditions were all that was needed to see if these things made a different.

Since the residents were beginning an improvement program one of their first major decisions was to improve the church building. The one room frame building built many years before underwent a transformation. It was brick veneered and five Sunday school rooms were added along with more windows. It was quite a transformation.

Throughout the community, mailboxes were given a coat of paint and names were stenciled on the boxes. They then were set on square posts that were painted black and white. In order that visitors would know when they entered Cash Point, signs were erected on the eastern and western boundaries. Side roads were marked and named.

New barns were built to take care of the increased crop yields and animals. Carpenters, plumbers, electricians and painters were kept busy remodeling and building homes. Residences were painted, electric pumps installed, bathrooms and kitchen sinks with running water were added so that the ladies of the house didn't have to use the old dish pans common in most farm houses.

When the contest was over in 1946, Cash Point won first place in the county and second in Middle Tennessee. The prize was $750. That prize gave the community incentive to continue working to improve the area, but already they were enjoying better living standards. In 1947, the Cash Point was awarded first place and won $1,000. By then the average attendance at community meetings was 187 with 75 families participating.

The group decided to tithe the prize money won the previous year and placed it in the church treasury. The church used this money to purchase a bulletin board and to improve the lawn. During this time, two large Sunday school rooms and a pastor's study were added to the main building, and a new roof, seats and foundation shrubbery were added. The pastor's library was equipped and a lending library started.

The Cash Point elementary school also received some attention. Fluorescent lights were installed, the grounds leveled and seeded, and the driveway graveled. Many will remember that driveway circled the front playground, and buses loaded and unloaded in front of the building each day.

Five and one-half miles of roadsides were spruced up with unsightly fence rows cleared and sloped with machinery.[17] A total of 2,600 acres of land was terraced and 36 drainage ditches were cut to drain the low, swampy land to allow for permanent pastures. When all the improvements were added in dollars and cents for 1947, the total reached the hundred thousand dollar mark. This was quite an achievement for a very small community, but it simply shows how focused they were and how they spared no effort in getting the job done.

The Cash Point Community committee traveled with Ray Ward logging 6,000 miles to tell their success story to others and spur them on to work for their own communities. TVA's W. M. Landress said at the time, "Without a doubt the Cash Point community in Lincoln County, did more to sell the idea of community improvements to county agents and other workers in the state and neighboring states, than any other community in Middle Tennessee." Each year, an annual tour was held to show hundreds of visitors the improvements in the community. Free barbecue dinners were served, and these were attended by between 300 and 600 people. Visitors from 38 states and eight foreign countries visited the area and put Cash Point on the map. Quite an achievement!

A movie was made available to other communities in the Tennessee Valley as well as throughout the U.S. and some foreign

---

[17] Looking Backward Through the Years, Nov. 1, 1952

countries. When asked how they did it, the answer was, "We caught a vision and worked individually and in cooperation."

The group didn't "rest on their laurels," but it continued to work together for years to improve the community. They set goals and worked diligently to accomplish those goals. During the years, they built a community club house that could be used by the church and school and organizations in the area. It was a 40x70 foot block building and was built entirely by donations from individuals, businesses and interested friends. The building when completed included a stage and kitchen. It was a welcome addition to the community and served it well until a number of years ago when the land was sold to someone from outside the area who used it for their own purposes.

But the loss of the community building today shouldn't take away from all the work and changes in Cash Point. By 1952, all families had electricity, washers, irons and refrigerators and 24 had indoor baths and several had home freezers. Crop yields improved as well. Corn yields increased from 20 to 60 bushels and cotton went to over a bale per acre. Milk sales increased to $60,000. Throughout the seven years until the Cash Point News was printed in 1952,[18] records showed that $163,364.88 had been spent for all buildings and repairs; $40,127.28 for home furnishings; $78,588.90 for electrical appliances; and $133,814.85 for farm machinery.

All this was done without government intercession. It was accomplished with guidance and knowledge from the extension agent and others, but the community supplied the labor and the money. This is definitely a model that any community can use to make improvements even today instead of relying on the state or federal government to come in and provide the cash and leadership. This is the way it is done when people get behind a project and diligently work toward the end product.

---

[18] Cash Point Community News, Nov. 1, 1952

Cleo and Ola Hicklen in a red clover field.

Bill and Harold Hargrave

Cash Point Community with Harvey Merrell's store on Right. Baugh Magnusson owned the grocery store on the left with the gas pumps during the 1940s and 1950s.

Nellie Ann Magnusson
Bryant and Children with
the Cash Point
Community Center in the
background.

George "Bitts" and Martha Hodges Hamilton family
Before they moved to Texas early 1900s

James Franklin Merrell and wife Margaret Gatlin Merrell

Geneva Ferguson (later Mrs. John Procak)

Ardmore, Needmore or Austin, It Was Still Home

Before the railroad came though Giles County, there was little to distinguish the area from many other settlements around. Trees, brush, wild animals, and wetlands were the only things to rest the eye on in those days. There were people living in the area, but travel was by horse and buggy or wagon, and quick runs were not made to the general store without a second's thought. Often the whole family traveled together, but that was no more than a few times a year.

People did move about. Farmers bought and sold land, moving their families to what they perceived to be a better location. Settlers moved into the area in in the early 1800s from the Carolinas, Virginia and numerous other places. They built log houses near creeks, added barns and enclosures to contain the animals, and then began to clear farm land.

The late Dr. Walter Johnson, a physician who grew up in the area, tells in his book entitled, *"The Things He Remembers,"* "I remember when the land on which this new bank building (Ardmore Branch of the First National Bank) stands was once covered by a pond, and the surrounding area was swampy, being the headwaters of Piney Creek. We used to hunt through these woods, and when I was a boy, there were turkey and wild deer here." Apparently some enterprising person(s) filled the pond and doubtlessly destroyed some of nature's wetlands in the process of draining the swamp. Such is the way of progress, but wetlands seldom totally give up, and one look at the area after a heavy rain will attest to that fact.

As early as the late 1800s, there were stores in the surrounding area. In Cash Point and in Elkmont Springs there were thriving communities already merging from the trees and undergrowth. In the area now known as Ardmore, a couple of individuals established stores or trading posts. One such merchant was Loss Watkins whose store stood about a quarter mile from the present Ardmore Methodist Church.[19] After Mr. Watkins quit his store, Mr. Tom Smith and his wife ran a small store just north of where the Methodist Church now stands.[20] Lonnie Ivy also ran a store on the 40 acres on which the Baptist parsonage was located, but

---

[19] "As I Remember It," by Odie Jones, 1979
[20] From an Interview with Mrs. F. C. Merrell, lifelong resident, (1903-1991)

later bought the 20 acres near the Tennessee state line and built a house and store at the Old Dee Boggs corner around 1907.

In a book entitled, *"As I remember It,"* Odie Jones says, "The Lonnie Ivy house and store were already there where Mr. Dee Boggs lives now in front of the Rainy Undertaker Establishment. Lonnie Ivy had already built telephone lines in the area before Ardmore was here."[21]

The Jones family home originally was near Piney Grove Church, an old log church building built in 1850. Mr. Jones describes the family home as a "little log house" built near a quick sand spring with thick woods everywhere. He also states there was a cotton gin near the house, but this was in Limestone County south of Ardmore. Mr. Jones spent his adult life in the Ardmore area, and witnessed the changes through the years.

Another merchant who predated Ardmore was Hubert Bess Mangum. His father Bill Mangum, a sawmill owner, moved to the Lonnie Ivy home and store about the time L&N announced its decision to build the railroad. Bill Mangum thus had the first sawmill in Ardmore, and his son, Hubert, a single man at the time went into business with him, according to Odie Jones.

When the Louisville and Nashville (L&N) Railroad announced plans to build a direct route from Nashville to Decatur, about 1910, Elkton merchant Alex Austin thought that where the railroad crossed the state line would be a good place to start a town, so he bought land on the Tennessee side and laid out lots. On this land, he built Austin's General Store sometime in 1911 just east of the railroad underpass (at or near where Lewter Hardware and Rochelle Hardware store operated for many years). Later he moved the store to what is now called West Town (just west of the underpass).

Austin mapped out lots in the future town and called it the Boyd-Austin-Childers subdivision. Lots were then offered for sale. At the time, the community began being called Austin, Mr. Jones states in his book, but when the railroad built the depot on the Alabama side, they named the

---

[21] "As I Remember It," by Odie Jones, 1979 (age at writing was 85)

place Ardmore. Although nothing has been found to substantiate the story, the late John Coats insisted Ardmore was called "Needmore" at one time.

Construction of the railroad brought a lot of foreigners to the area, and they were certainly noticed. Fountain Clay Merrell, a lad of four or five years at the time and a life-long resident before his death in 1986 told of hearing the men speaking in a foreign language. It made quite an impression on the young boy. He also remembered the first train that rain on July 8, 1914. "Herman, Pitts and I (brothers) were laying flat on our backs with typhoid fever when the first train ran. We heard the whistle and sure did want to see it," he wrote in a family history in 1978.[22] No doubt that first train was just as exciting to that generation as the first man on the moon was to a much later generation in the Tennessee Valley.

Ardmore Depot

The John Wesley Parker family was early residents on the Alabama side, and their daughter Zelma Parker lived at the residence on what is now 6th Street until she passed away. Her mother was Martha H. Smith Parker. The Parkers lived at Union Hill prior to moving to Ardmore. Miss Zelma a retired school teacher said in an interview, "I remember my

---

[22] The History of the Tennessee Branch of the Merrell Family, 1978

mother telling Mrs. Bill Mangum, there might a town here someday." Needless to say the elder Mrs. Parker was correct.

Ardmore hasn't had many who left to seek fame and fortune, but certainly there have been successful people who came out of this area. Miss Parker indicated that tradition says Andrew Jackson raced horses just south of Ardmore. A race track was built near the old underpass south of town, and Jackson was reported to have stopped on occasion to race his horse. If it is true, unfortunately, there is no record of this story.

Soon after the railroad was completed, businesses began to spring up in Ardmore. Tom White, Bee Bottom and Flournoy Douthit built a large brick building near the old depot. At the time Ft. Hampton Road (now Main Street) and Railroad Street were the main roads in town. Bricks used to make the store building were fired in a kiln owned by White. According to Mr. Odie Jones, "White and Bottoms had a store in one and Flournoy Douthit had a store in the other." [23] In the 1940s, Ardmore Telephone Company was located upstairs over the White store, and it remained there until it was moved to a new building across from the drug store in the early 1950s. It remained in that building until 1957 when it was moved to the current location by F. C. Merrell.

Where Rainey Funeral Home was built, Garrett Whitt built a kiln, but according to Mr. Jones, it was not successful. Toney Rainey and Jim Rainey operated the funeral home for years beginning in 1930. Later it was sold to Don Taylor who later moved it further east on Highway 53. It later became Ardmore Memorial Funeral Home, but it closed after a few years. The current funeral home is Ardmore Chapel Funeral Home.

The first restaurant in Ardmore was owned by Hubert Mangum. Mangum whose first store was located out in the county on Cedar Hill Road at the Brown/Whitt corner and later the Dee Boggs corner, then moved to the area west of Railroad Street where Joe Rollin's plumbing was later located. The restaurant was apparently in the back of his store. In 1923 Mangum moved his grocery store once again – this time to what is now Ardmore Avenue, down toward the old bus station and across from the Bledsoe/Bryan home. His son Reynard operated the store for years.

---

[23] "As I Remember It," by Odie Jones, 1979

John Toone had the first barbershop in Ardmore, and haircuts were 10 cents with shaves costing five cents.

Though many may think Jones Drug was the first to spring up in Ardmore, it wasn't. Lewd Currin and Dr. Woodard built the first drug store in Ardmore, and Woodard was the first doctor to locate in the new community. Another early doctor was Dr. W.S. Mims, father of Brown and Morgan Mims. Later doctors who practiced in Ardmore were Dr. John Baugh Maddox, Dr. Daniel T. Hardin and Dr. Clyde Marshall. According to Odie Jones, the Currin-Woodard Drug Store was struck by lightning after it was newly built and opened. He doesn't say if it was destroyed, but sometime in the 1920s, a bad storm hit the area and burned several buildings on what was Railroad Street. Mrs. Zelma Parker recalled, "It was raining and folks carried water, but they couldn't put out the fire." It is likely the drugstore was one of those burned. Later a Mr. Gallasspi (or Gillespie) ran a drug store in Ardmore. Finally, Ardmore Drug Store was built, and it is still in business today as Jones Drug Store.

The first cotton gin was owned by M. Y. Douthit, according to Odie Jones, it was located on the main street about where Western Auto was located.[24] Other early businesses included a blacksmith shop owned by George Elder, a shoe shop owned by Will Rolin, garages owned by Sherman Ferguson and Jesse Mitchell, a car dealership owned by Bryce White, a grist mill owned by Gauthney and Downing and a hotel owned by W. D. Buchanan. Goodloe Jones served as the first undertaker before Toney Rainey moved to Ardmore from Blanche. Pug Johnson owned a garage in Ardmore in the 1950s, possibly earlier than that.

First Baptist Church can claim the honor of having been the first church established in Ardmore. It was founded in 1915.[25] Before the church was established, tent meetings were held by Rev. H. C. Smith and Rev. J. V. Kirkland. At a meeting on April 15, 1915, the church was organized and families included W. F. Mangum, F. M. Whitt and J. W. Parker. A wooden building was built and the congregation moved into the building in November of that same year.

---

[24] As I Remember It by Odie Jones, 1979
[25] First Baptist Church, Ardmore, TN official webpage

Following a fire in March 1947 that destroyed the wooden church, a new building was erected. This building was sold to the city of Ardmore, AL and is now the town hall. The current church was built in 1991.

Serving as pastors during the history of the church were the following: H. C. Smith, W. W. Jones, S.S. Hacker, W. T. Cobb, J. B. Alexander, B. E. Franklin, Hudson Hicks, L. M. Laten, Lucius Hart, Ewell Sexton, J. T. Hart, M. H. Willingham, F. W. Walker, J. T. Camp, J. W. Meadows, V. T. Lewis, M.O. Blackwelder, E. D. Doris, Robert Couch, James Rolison, Wheeler Kidd, Paul Clutts, Sammie Brister, Chris Barnett, Paul Mason and Alan Hughes.[26]

Football in Ardmore has been around for many years. The first football and basketball coach at Ardmore was B. Earl Graham, a Birmingham Southern graduate. His team won five games, lost three and tied one for the season. Julius Magnusson was the first football captain with team members including a Whitt, Jones, Forbes, Eastman and Broadway.

Clint Van Hoozer had the first cream station in the area for farmers to sell their cream. This was in the 1920s. Later Ardmore Creamery was established and run by Thoran Jones.

Other firsts were Thomas Garrett who was the first photographer and many years later, A. C. Austin opened the first movie theater – Fox Theater – which served the general public for many years. In the 1950s and possibly later, Robert Hargrove was a photographer in Ardmore.

Ardmore has never had much public transportation. However, Lewd Currin did run a taxi service in Ardmore in its early years using his private vehicle to transport people from Ardmore to Athens, the county seat for those on the Alabama side of the state line. Currin also sold Essex automobiles in Ardmore, Athens and Pulaski in the 1920s. Another similar transportation service was run by Walter Neaves, and Rainy Funeral Home at one time used their vehicles as ambulances to transport patients until new laws prohibited them from operating an emergency medical service. Of course, Greyhound Bus Station operated in Ardmore for many years

---

[26] Ardmore Baptist Church History, official web site

under the guidance of Mrs. Tennie Bledsoe. L&N also had passenger cars stopping in Ardmore in the 1940s.

Ardmore acquired the nickname Suds City in the 1940s and '50s because of the taverns on the Tennessee side. Jack Houck owned the first tavern in Ardmore. It was located on the south side of Main Street near the underpass and when people finished their beers, they could play tennis behind the tavern. There have been a number of taverns in and around Ardmore on the Tennessee side since that original one built in the 1930s - Bloody Bucket, Steadman's Giles County Tavern, Coxes, 31 Blue Spot, Valley Tavern and Garon's and probably others. Through the years, there were numerous other businesses in Ardmore. These played a major role in the economy of the area and were a great asset to the local residents.

As late as the 1940s and 1950s, Ardmore's East Main Street was a tree lined and several homes stood there. These homes were torn down to make way for businesses through the years, and today there is little evidence of their having been there. Mr. Harrison Mullins was one of the residents who lived on the main street. He was principal of Ardmore High School for a number of years and later taught at Blanche.

While there weren't many places to go for entertainment or to dine in Ardmore during the mid-century, residents did enjoy a few events. Carnivals came to town yearly, tent meetings were held down near the old railroad tunnel south of town, and films were showed out of doors and projected on buildings. However, what really brought people to town were the Saturday drawings that merchants held by the depot in the 1950s. People came from the four surrounding counties to participate in the drawings. There were always winners for the cash prizes and other giveaways.

When the Fox Theater came to town, Wednesday nights was the big draw. The theater ran a movie and held a drawing, which no doubt filled the theater on those nights. The Singing Wheels Skating Rink also drew the young people to town, and there is no telling how many miles the kids skated by going round and round that rink each night. Unfortunately, the Fox Theater was sold by A. C. Austin, and adult movies became the fare for several years. Today Ardmore has no theater or skating rink.

Although settled by moral, law abiding people, Ardmore has at times suffered from a less than spotless reputation, which can be said for most any city, town or community. A tavern called Bloody Bucket, later kown as 31 Blue Spot, was opened after Houck's place closed, and legends it that after a session of drinking, folks would often be thrown out the windows of this establishment. Ardmore gained the nickname of Suds City and was known far and wide in the surrounding area by that name. The name, obviously, referred to the taverns operating on the Tennessee side.

Shady characters often found their way to Ardmore and sullied its good name, and as is often the case, bad news travels faster than good. Such was the case in Ardmore at times, but Ardmore is still a good place to live and raise a family. Whether it was Ardmore, Austin, Needmore or Suds City Ardmore is still home to most that grew up there.

One incident about Ardmore involved the building of Ardmore High School.[27] One headline read: "Badge W. Whitt, Prominent Merchant and Citizen of Ardmore Shot Down by Morrell Brothers." "Again the deadly pistol has been used in its work, and two citizens are in the county jail awaiting the outcome of their murderous assault upon one of the leading citizens of this county.

"Late Friday afternoon about half-past three o'clock, the streets of Ardmore was the scene of a bloody encounter, when Jake and Ed Morrell, brothers residing near that village, shot Mr. Badge W. Whitt, a leading businessman and citizen of Ardmore, five times, nine shots in all it is said being fired by the Morrell's at the wounded man, several after he had fallen to the ground, he was shot both in front and in the back , five bullets entering his body.

"The trouble all came up over the school house question. Mr. Whitt was one of the men who was foremost in the establishment of the splendid brick school building at Ardmore, and the Morrell's were of the small faction that opposed the location of the school at the growing village of Ardmore, and have been very severe in their talk and actions about the school since its location there. This led up to the unfortunate encounter in

---

[27] Athens News Courier, Athens, AL, July 26, 1926

which a good man and enterprising citizen may lose his life. Just how the trouble started is not determined as we hear several sides to the affair, but all of the reports lead to the end that the wounded man was fired upon by the Morrell's without any excuse.

"He was approaching them; it is said, asking for a friendly discussion of some matter, when they both opened fire on him with revolvers which they drew from their clothes. He was unarmed and was astonished at their action but unable to defend himself as they opened fire.

"It is said that these men were in Athens on Saturday before the trouble and each purchased a pistol. They evidently were fixing for something of this sort. At last account about six o'clock, the Morrell brothers reached Athens and surrendered to the sheriff and are in jail, awaiting the outcome of their work before they can obtain a preliminary trial. The people of Ardmore are greatly distressed over this unfortunate and unnecessary shooting, as it leaves a blotch on the good name of the prosperous and growing community.

"Mr. Whitt is a member of one of the oldest and most prominent families of that section. The Whitt's have long been known for their probity (decency) and high standing and none of them have ever been engaged in any brawl or unlawful conduct.

"The Courier hopes that his excellent citizen may pull through and be spared to his family." (*Editor's note: Whitt did survive the shooting. He was married first and second to two McKenny sisters and lastly to Docia Gatlin. His legs were paralyzed for life. The Morrell's served time in jail for their crime. Badge was the father of 12 children and died in 1942 at the age of 80.*)

Ardmore Depot construction in 1909. The depot closed on Dec. 10, 1965. [28] (Photo Courtesy of Sherry Newman)

---

[28] The Pulaski Citizen, Dec. 8, 196537

Faces and Places of Yesterday

Ardmore High School's first girls' basketball team: Members were Marceal Willingham, Doris Neaves, Margaret Hastings, Adora Mims, Marie Smith, Frances McDonald, Margarette Merrell, Gladys Colston, and Martha Dean Lewter. (Photo courtesy of Beverly McConnell Browning)

Local Teens at the Quick and Tasty (Gail McDonald, and others (Photo courtesy of Beverly Browning/Duane Berry)

38

Fountain C. Merrell & Margarette Merrell about 1950
at Ardmore Telephone Company across from the drug store.

**Blue & Gray Café in Ardmore, AL built and owned by T.C., Doug and Jim
McDonald.** Thomas and Dorothy Merrell operated this café briefly in the late
1950s.

Faces and Places of Yesterday

George Washington Merrell Home near Union Hill Church in Giles Co.
The home is no longer owned by the family.

Fred and Harold "Buddy" Stevenson, both AHS Graduates and veterans of
WWII. Fred worked for the Army in Huntsville. Buddy was a veterinarian.

Faces and Places of Yesterday

Terrell, Annis Merrell Godwin, Elden and Trudy Crabtree Merrell

Quick and Tasty as it was being built by Vernon Hardy and Charlie Berry
(Photo courtesy of Duane Berry)

AHS High School Band, Main Street (photo courtesy Beverly Browning)

Quick and Tasty with carhop on duty (courtesy Duane Berry)

Faces and Places of Yesterday

Mrs. Malcum (Sue) Smith with Charlie Mullins house in background. The frame house once belonged to Mr. "Dink" Barnett. The brick home on the right is the Cash Point Church parsonage [29]

Members of the Barnett Family
Ed, Della, Elzie, John, Jessie. Pernie and Deimer Barnett

[29] Photo and information courtesy of Peggy Holt

43

Sally Hamilton who married Lewis Mitchell
(Courtesy Kenneth Smith)

Curtis Merrell and wife Bette Merrell in Lawndale, CA
He was the son of Herman D. and Corrine Merrell

Rhonda Merrell 1940-1986
Daughter of Lewis & Mary Merrell

Clay Merrell, USAF, about 1949-50
Son of Fountain and Dealie Merrell

Faces and Places of Yesterday

Loretta, Marge, Clay, Orlean, Marie and Thomas Merrell at Clingman's Dome in the Smoky Mountains early 1940's.

Faye & Bill Hand celebrating their 45th Anniversary at Cash Point Baptist Church. They were the first couple to be married in the new church in January 1964.

Loretta and Bob Ekis December 18, 1959 after their wedding at
Northside Baptist Church in Huntsville, AL

**Archie Kathrine Arnett Merrell and Franklin
Pitts Merrell**

47

Faces and Places of Yesterday

Marie & Howard Broadway celebrating their 50th Anniversary
Held In 1992 in Martin, TN at First Baptist Church

Robert W. Ekis, WWII 1943   **Howard Broadway WWII 1943**
101st Airborne   **U.S. Army Infantry**

Mrs. Lou Hargrave and Sons Edward, Milton who is looking over Bill's shoulder, Hilliard, Johnny, Wendell and Raymond Hargrave.

Fountain C. Merrell on a telephone pole, Ardmore, TN about 1950 on Highway 110 just east of Rainey Funeral Home – This photo gives a good idea of what the area looked like before Highland Heights was built.

Dealie & Fountain C. Merrell about 1940

BHS Class of 1926 - Some of the names of the students, not necessarily in order are: Virginia Merrell, M. Rainey, L. Maddox, Mildred Twitty, M. Renolds, M. Hardin, M. McDaniel, O. McLemore, Mr. Carroll (far left second row), R. Vickers, L. McDaniel, W. Tucker, Lucille Hall, R. Hardin, a Bishop, L. Robinson, B. Brock, D. McDaniel, a Miss Everly, L. Colbert, S. Flanagan, J. Watson, G. Davidson and A. Commons.

This House is the former home of James F. and Margaret Gatlin Merrell on Merrell Road. It was built about 1909. It was purchased by the Randolph Family and is still owned by that family.

The Fountain C. Merrell Family about 1965

LETTERS FROM OUR SOLDIER BOYS[30]

Lewis H. Merrell's Letter to His Brother
Herman Merrell

Ward T. Wilson War Hospital
Reading, England

Dear Brother,

I will try to drop you a few lines in answer to letter of Oct. 10th, and which I was real glad to hear from you, and more than glad to know that you had not left the U. S. at that time. So I feel good with the hope that you are still in New Jersey and peace has come and you missed the bloody risk of your life over here that so many of us endured.

I am well and happy after all my good luck, which I suppose you have heard of long ago. I was in a scrap with old Jerry September 29 and got shot through my right arm below the elbow, and the next day they took it off three inches above the elbow. It wasn't a bullet wound, but a 5-9 shrapnel, which is many times worse. But, listen; I'm proud to be living today and I've given my right arm freely for a cause that is right and just. So why should I worry? No, not all, for I have another one left. I'm most well now, having a good time and expect to leave here soon to step on a steamer for the United States. I am longing for the day to come when we can be back home together again, aren't you? Well, Bud, I could tell you some interesting stories, but I get tired writing left handed, so I will wait until I return home and tell you better than I can write. I hope you are having a good time, and remember and have one for us both Christmas. Will close with best wishes that you are well and receive this, and also that we may be at home together soon.

Your Brother in England,
Lewis H. Merrell

---

[30] This letter was published in the Fayetteville Observed on Dec. 19, 1918

Thomas E. Merrell, U. S. Army about 1953

AHS Coaches Eugene Cooper and Harold Murrell
(Photo courtesy Beverly Browning)
54

John and Fanta Edwards

Sim E. and Hazel Merrell Smith

Children of Fountain and Dealie Merrell, 1938, L to R, Clay, Marge, Marie holding Loretta, Orlean and Thomas.

Sarah Francis Mitchell

Cotton Picking Time in Cash Point

Clyde (Pete) and Mary Lou Hamilton Franklin

Dealie Ferguson, about 1912-13

Sarah Jane and John Sherrell Ferguson. She was the daughter of Henry Clay Hamilton and Amanda Bonner Hamilton. He was the son of William Wood Ferguson and Margaret Mabin Ferguson. The Ferguson/Mabin family came from Chester County South Carolina originally.

Marge and son Mark McConnell, 1963

**Harold Hargrave, holding Peggy, wife Velma Clark Hargrave
with son Gayland in back.**

Cass Smith and Ola Hicklen

Cash Point Baptist Pastorium

Joe Roper Grocery with Joe on the right, unknown male on left

Cash Point Vacation Bible School 1950s

Cash Point Elementary School 3rd-5th Grades 1952

Bro. Kennedy baptizing in a creek in 1944

Tombstone of Robert Clovis Smith in the Smith Family Cemetery Near the Malone Cemetery. (courtesy Faye Hand)

Faces and Places of Yesterday

Scene in Ardmore about 1940's to early 1950's.
Car on the left appears to be the one owned by Pete and Mary Lou Franklin.

A 1940s quilting bee at the Woodman of the World Building in Cash Point.
L to R, 1st row, Alma Brown, Maggie Slayton, Annie Smith, Verona Smith, Hazel Smith, Ruth Franklin, Mildred Whitman, holding a small girl; Mary Franklin, Zelia Magnusson, Eliza Barnett, Annis Lou Mitchell holding Patricia Mitchell and Alma Roper; 2nd row, Fannie Jester, unknown, Louise Smith, maybe Agnes Bayless, Lucille Mitchell or Earlene Tuck?, Lucille Maddox, Shirley Jones, Mattie Bee Franklin, unknown, Stella Barnett, Annie Lee Ferguson, unknown, Nannie Smith; 3rd Row, Golda Roper Harris, Geneva Hargrove, Sarah Mitchell, unknown maybe Annie Hargrave, Annie Merrell, Alberta Smith, Affie May Franklin, Leota Roper, unknown, Iona Roper, Eula Barnett, Minnie Barnett, Ethel Hamilton, unknown, Mrs. Elzie Barnett.

Class of 1929 Cash Point School – front, Garland Whitt, Verona Hicklen, Hazel Merrell, Mary Lou Hamilton, and Myron Rogers; back, John F. Spray teacher; Elmer Roper, Malcom Tomerlin and Herbert Slayton.

Gayland Hargrave and Mrs. Ethel Ferguson 1955

Faces and Places of Yesterday

Old Time Days held in 1983

Seated is Mrs. Ada Burns with Brenda Smith, Stella Barnett, Hazel Smith, Lucille Gatlin, Allene Roper, Joe Roper, Minnie Mae and T.L. Ferguson;, second row, unknown, Bobby Barnett, Gayland Hargrave; Steve Gibson holding Jenny, Oscar Barnett, Coy Barnett, Paulette Mitchell, Josephine Mitchell, Peggy Holt, Bro. Bill Suddarth and Karen Holt.

Cash Point Vacation Bible School about 1956

Faces and Places of Yesterday

Thomas Ed Merrell about 1985

Ladies Sunday school Class at Cash Point with Brother Kennedy

**Clint Van Hoozer and mother Mary Jane
Van Hoozer** (photo courtesy Laurene Schrimsher)

Logan Smith
69

Cash Point Church Dinner in the 1970s

Avis Henderson's SS Class at Cash Point late 1950s
Betty Barnett, Fay Hicklen, Reba Hicklen, Patsy Smith, unknown, Verna Fay
Lewter, Faye Merrell, Mrs. Henderson, Doris Holt, Peggy Hargrave

Faces and Places of Yesterday

Mock Wedding at Cash Point Community Center – T.B. and Sarah Mitchell, Kathleen Henderson, Marion Hicks, Gayland Hargrave and Rabon Bayless

Another Mock Wedding - Starring Bro. Glen Hester, Freddie Smith, Wayne Henderson, Cass Smith, Harold and Jeanette Owen

Still another Mock Wedding – Starring Tommy Hargrove, Iona roper, Lucille Gatlin and Betty Smith

Note Burning at Cash Point Church in 1948

Mattie Bea Franklin and Ruth and Luther Franklin

Allene Roper and Children Play in the Snow at Cash Point

Cash Point Baptist Church singers – Joyce Mitchell, Bobby Barnett, Donald Owen, Calvin and Peggy Holt

Martha Roper Riley widow of Andrew Ferrell Riley and unknown grandchildren (Photo Courtesy Kenneth Smith)

Neil and Cythnia A. Paysinger Smith – Grandparents of Cornelius (Dooley) Coffman. (Courtesy of Kenneth Smith)

Lewis C. and Sally Hamilton Mitchell (Photo courtesty Kenneth Smith)

John B Mitchell holding Vergie, Minnie holding Pitts, with Elsie standing (Photo courtesy Kenneth Smith)

Herman Dale Merrell, WWI

Faces and Places of Yesterday

Sim and Hazel Merrell Smith's 50th Wedding Anniversary
Ray, Bettye, Hazel, Sim, Anna and Harmon Smith

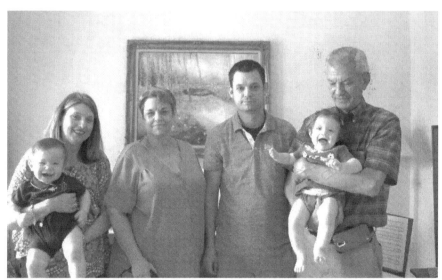

The Harmon Smith family, from left, Jennifer, Susan, Michael, Harmon, and twins Jason and Laura. Susan is the daughter of singer George Jones. The family lives near Nashville, TN

77

Barnett Family
Elzie, "Dink", Deimer, Ann; back row, Mae; Della, John and Pernie. Mae, who died at age 24, is the grandmother of Peggy Hargrave Holt

Faye Merrell about 1962 in Huntsville, AL

Faces and Places of Yesterday

Cash Point honored their seniors with a special dinner in the 1950's
Attending were: seated Ida Smith, Millie Lewter, Madden Smith, Garthie Slayton, Evie Jones, Bertha Maddox, Herman Maddox; standing mid-section, Ed Barnett, Asa Merrell, Jim Maddox, Eva Puckett, Minnie Barnett, Lou Hargrave, Lula Tillery (peering over Mrs. Lou's head), Koy Smith, Maggie Rodgers, Essie Merrell, Fannie Jester, Eula Barnett and Alma Roper; back row, Theo Maddox and Grady Smith, behind these two and higher up are John Tillery, Lucille Maddox Lee Rodgers, Mrs. Smith (Nellie Kennedy's mother), Brother Raymond Kennedy, John Barnett and Johnny Maddox.

So many are gone from this community, but hopefully these photos will help you remember them.

Harold Owen, center stage, playing his favorite role.

Asa and Jenny Merrell

Faces and Places of Yesterday

Oscar and Eva Bell Currin

Dinner at Cash Point Baptist Church for Bro. Hester

Seated are Peggy Holt, Marion Hicks, Bro Glen Hester, Joan Hester, Allene Roper, Jeannette Owen, Aline Hargrove, Gene Paul Currin; standing Jean Lewter, Jean Hicks, Bill Hand, Faye Hand, Calvin Holt, Joe Roper, Harold Owen, Tommy Hargrove, Betty Currin, Beatrice Barnett, Kathleen Henderson

Lewis H. Merrell, WWI
He served his country faithfully as did his brother Herman D. Merrell. Lewis saw duty in Europe and lost his right arm, but the loss never stopped him from doing the things he really wanted to do.

Faces and Places of Yesterday

Ardmore High School Twirlers – 1966
L to R: Barbara Bartlett, Shana Shannon, Curtis Bryant, Judy Whitt and Beverly
McConnell (photo courtesy Beverly Browning)

Mrs. Annie Sherrell Holland and some of her music students
(Photo courtesy Beverly Browning)

Faces and Places of Yesterday

AHS Marching Band about 1970 – Main Street
Mrs. Barbara Bartlett in vehicle on right. (Photo courtesy Beverly Browning)

Ardmore Marching Band early 1960s
Curtis Bryant was drum major; majorettes were Beverly McConnell, Shana
Shannon and Barbara Bartlett. (Photo courtesy of Beverly Browning)

The Marvin Holt Family

Garrett Merrell Jr, aka "Cann" Merrell
Son of Garrett Merrell and Amy Walker Merrell

Faces and Places of Yesterday

John Whitt and Mary Polly Merrell Whitt
(daughter of Garrett Merrell and Olive Thompson Merrell

Jemima Merrell Puckett wife of John Washington Puckett.
She was born in 1837 daughter of Garrett & Olive Thompson Merrell

Kelly's Creek Community

Who were the first settlers in Kelly's Creek? It's difficult to say since the area was settled earlier than the start of the Baptist Church there. But some of the people who have surfaced in this author's genealogy research indicate that the Mitchell, Hamilton, Bonner, Reed, McRee, Smith, Rawls, Ferguson, Brown, Mullins, Philpot, White, Hall, Heard, O'Neal, Owens, Leatherwood, Mitchell, Griffis and other families settled in that area early on.

Kelly's Creek is not a town but a community that centers around the Baptist Church and creek that runs through the area. The creek itself starts at Blanche and continues west to the Elk River near Baugh in Giles County. John Kelly owned the land in that area before 1817, and is thought to one of the first settlers. It is commonly held that the community received its name from John Kelly.[31]

At one time, Kelly's Creek was a thriving community with gins, a grist mill and stores that operated at various times. Known businesses were stores owned by the Mitchells, Philpots. Lewis Ferguson also owned a store there as did Tricky Jim Smith. Sam Hall ran a store called Loafers' Joy and there was a Mullins and Heard grocery near the county line. Elections were held for many years at the Philpot store, but they later moved to the front yard of the Philpot's home where they were held until 1946 when elections moved to the Mullins store.

A water spout formed at the headwaters of Kelly's Creek on July 12, 1885, and destroyed fields on both sides of the creek as well as the Rawls and Griffis mills. Nathan Smith's wheat and fencing were swept away and lumber wagons from the Owens and Leatherwood's saw mill were carried away by the current. J. S. Merrell also suffered losses at his farm. Dr. Beck's mare drowned during that event, and Mr. Eph White's wife was thunder shocked. Later on June 29, 1929, Kelly's Creek also reached flood stage and washed away Ferguson's store.

In 1942, Kelly's Creek Baptist church had the misfortune of losing the church's roof during a "cyclone."

---

[31] Lincoln County Tennessee Homecoming '86 publication

Faces and Places of Yesterday

A school was located near the church before 1900, but after it closed children were sent to Elk Ridge School. Later children from this community attended Cash Point and Blanche Schools.

William Rodgers, a resident of the community, served as Lincoln County Sheriff in 1894 and 1895.

Though many of the younger generation do not remember this next interesting tidbit, Kelly's Creek native, James Neal (Bull) Brown, son of Neal and Minnie Brown, attended school at Blanche and Morgan in Petersburg, TN, before enrolling in Vanderbilt. Brown received all American honors in football in the late 1920's at Vanderbilt.[32]

The Kelly's Creek Home Demonstration Club organized in May 1933 and elected Mrs. Cora Henderson as president. Other members included Aileen Smith and Mabel Mitchell.

The community could claim three century farms in 1976. They belonged to H. D. Hill, Monroe Hill and W. F. Philpot. Each received county and state certificates.

James Franklin "Tricky Jim" Smith[33] was a prosperous farmer in Lincoln County, TN. He was born in 1835 to Lemuel and DeBolious Birmingham Smith in Kelly's Creek. Tricky Jim's family moved to Madison County, AL when he was in his teens and then to Limestone County. When Tricky Jim was 17, he began working for the Alabama Courier. His first written work for the Courier was his father's obituary in 1854. Tricky Jim was 19 years old then. When the Civil War broke out, he joined the Confederate Army, but only stayed in for a little while.

Jim's brother Pinkney died around 1855 and left a widow and 2 sons. After coming home from the war, Tricky Jim found his sister-in-law had been committed to the insane asylum in Tuscaloosa, AL where she died in July 1877. Tricky Jim took in his nephew Lawson and raised him as his his own son. What happened to the other son is unknown. Lawson married Sarah Ann Browning in 1878.

---

[32] Lincoln County Tennessee Homecoming '86
[33] The story of Tricky Jim Smith is taken from The Smith Family history by Kenneth Smith.

Tricky Jim and his sister, Sarah, along with Lawson moved back to Lincoln County and bought a farm on the north ridge overlooking the south side of Kelly's Creek. Tricky Jim continued to live on his 371 acre farm until his death.

Tricky Jim opened a store on his farm in 1879 and named the store "Tricky" from a nickname given to him early in his life. Tricky Jim's store carried dry goods, hardware, seeds, farm equipment and later on fertilizer when it was introduced in the late 1890s. Jim not only ran a store, but loaned money to neighbors, speculated in land, and when necessary took debtors to court who would not repay their debt. His farm was later owned by Nolen Holt, and Cecil Holland owned the land where the store stood.

Many stories were told about Tricky Jim and his money. It is probably part fact and part fiction, but the stories have caused people to search his farm for gold. One of the reasons was because he told that he could sit in his kitchen and see where his gold was hidden. He did own property on which he had several tenant houses, so Tricky Jim probably did have money, but no one has ever found money that was supposed to have been buried on his farm. Tricky Jim Smith died in 1914.

In the early days, throughout the area, women had to spin cotton and wool, form cloth on a loom, and then sew clothing from the whole cloth. Knitting was also an essential skill. Pioneer women in Kelly's Creek were no exception to the rule. The women cooked using pots hung above or standing on the fireplace. Coffee was often made from okra, rye and parched corn. Coffee beans that were imported did not often appear in the home. Lighting was by candle or by oil lamps. Electricity did not make its way into S.W. Lincoln County until the 1930's and 1940's.

Leather for shoes, shirts and pants came from hides of animals the men hunted. There were no gasoline motors, or gas for that matter, so all plowing and planting was done with a mule, horse or ox, and women as well as children participated in the planting. If you were lazy during those early years, you wouldn't have eaten. That was life in the late 19th century and very early 20th century.

One prominent family in Kelly's Creek was the O'Neal Family. Thomas Jefferson O'Neal was the head of this family. He married Sarah Jane Bonner who died in 1918. Thomas J. O'Neal served in the Civil War for the Confederate States of America. His children were Mary Jane, W.P. (Bill), James Willis and Ann Thomas. Ann never knew her father who died before she was born. The family intermarried with Smith, Paysinger, and other local families. Thomas was killed during the Civil War.

Kelly's Creek Baptist Church of Christ, from one incomplete record in the author's possession, began to form about 1865. The document shows H. R. Bray and G. W. Puckett's names on the constitution, but they are typewritten and no date is filled in. Perhaps the earliest minutes were lost because the next minutes of the church begin in 1880 some 15 years later. These records were faithfully copied and presented to the Lincoln County Genealogical Society by H. Russell O'Neal.[34]

The first record is recorded for June 2, 1880 and indicates the church held preaching by Bro. J. W. Hillrand (sic) on the text, "Grieve Not the Holy Spirit of God, whereby ye are sealed until the day of Redemption." That day, the church appointed Hillrand (sic) as the moderator of the church, went into session, and called Hillrand (sic) to the pastorate for an indefinite period of time. The entry was signed by J. W. Hilliard, MD and J. S. Merrell, CC. (editor's note: it is unclear if there is a typo in the Hillrand name, and that it is actually Hilliard. It does appear that the Hillrand who is preaching is J. W. Hilliard, MD in the later entries.

Bro. Hilliard continued to serve as pastor until he was taken ill in August 1886, at which time F. M. Yeager stepped in to serve as moderator.

In the late 1880s, church members were held to high standards, and when one was found stepping outside the boundaries of good conduct, they were either called before the church to answer for their actions and/or to ask forgiveness. In November 1886, J. Moore asked the church to forgive him for getting drunk. The church also collected $12 from the congregation to purchase a heating stove—the two actions not related.

Various charges in the late 1800's were brought against members of the congregation for conduct unbecoming a Christian, which included drinking and swearing, dancing, and other miscellaneous things. These charges of indiscretion were sometimes answered at the next meeting, but

---

[34] Kelly Creek Baptist Church of Christ, H. Russell O'Neal

sometimes the person charged would not show up and simply quit attending church. When the person did show, they were usually forgiven and restored to fellowship. These records were maintained during the 1880's and 1890s. What happened afterwards is not a part of the file copied by Russell O'Neal.

In February, W. Smith brought charges against A. Van Hoozer for conduct unbecoming a Christian. Van Hoozer was excluded from the church.[35]

Once again in April 1887, J. Moore was brought up before the church for intoxication and swearing. Two members were appointed to talk to him, that being J. Smith and J. Merrell. At the next meeting, the committee reported to the church and the charges were dropped. However, G. Whitt wasn't so fortunate, it seems. At the same meeting J. Smith brought charges against G. Whitt for intoxication and swearing, and the church withdrew fellowship from him. The record states there was considerable discussion about non-fellowship, but "they was allowed until next stated meeting." The record does not indicated any follow up action in the next meeting.

In January 1888, L. J. Bledsoe stated the church was not in fellowship, and charges were brought against the following: W. Smith, C. Rowell, A. Paysinger, and D. Gatlin.[36] Two committees were appointed to speak with the persons. Charges were also levied by B. Smith against J. McGuire, J. Whitt and L. Gatlin for drunkenness and dancing. [37]

The following month, the unstated charges against A. Paysinger and D. Gatlin were upheld, but they would not acknowledge their conduct. In the case of W. Smith and C. Rowell, Rowell would not acknowledge the charge and W. Smith denied the charge. Smith was restored to fellowship. J. Whitt would not acknowledge and was excluded. L. Gatlin's charges were to be considered at a later date.

---

[35] The names are listed in the church records.
[36] Kelly's Creek Baptist Church minutes, Russell O'Neal
[37] Kelly's Creek Baptist Church recorded meeting minutes, Russell O'Neal

It is interesting that such charges were brought, and one must consider if some of these charges may not have been deserved? Only the people involved at that time knew, but at that particular time in history, apparently church members did hold one another to very high standards. Probably not always a bad thing, but most would agree that being called before the congregation and charged with bad conducted would have been a humbling experience. Sometimes charges could be levied for nothing more than not attending church. Imagine if that were the case today! There would be many notes in the church records, to be sure.

These members were no better or worse than anyone else in the surrounding communities. Kelly's Creek Baptist Church, today, is no doubt very similar to all area Baptist Churches. These old records were included only for their historical value not as a blanket condemnation of the church or its members.

Today, Kelly's Creek Baptist Church strives to see that all people saved and lost alike know the story of their Lord and Savior Jesus Christ. The doors are open and visitors are always welcome.

Lessie Alice Puckett & Eugene M. Weeks,
At their wedding, Oct. 1904

James Madison Puckett and Hannah Cora Hall,
At Union Hill Church

Sherrell Austin, left, son of John Austin and Stella Ferguson Austin, lived in Limestone County most of his life. He had a brother J. D. Austin who was named for his father, John D. Austin., and sisters Myrtle who married Homer Bates and Clara who married Bunyon Brock.

93

**Kathrine Orlean Merrell and Josephine
Mitchell,** early 1940's

Aulene Smith Puckett
She was the wife of Malcum Puckett
And mother of Malcum Jr., and Susan

Faces and Places of Yesterday

**Union Hill Baptist Church, old building above and newer below
(Photos courtesy of Laurene Schrimsher)**

Faces and Places of Yesterday

John Willard Campbell and Malcum Puckett
at a Merrell Reunion 1990's

Elkmont Springs Hotel about 1920's (photo courtesy Laurene Schrimsher)

96

Faces and Places of Yesterday

Herman Merrell surrounded by nieces and nephews:
Front row, left to right, Clay, Thomas and Loretta Merrell; Back
left to right, Annis, Orlean, Herman, Marie and Marge Merrell, about 1940

Joel W. Ekis who lived in the area
a couple of years, but no book would be
complete without including the author's son
since his maternal forefathers came from the area.

Isaac Gatlin and Ruby Bond Gatlin
Ruby was the second wife of Isaac. He was
the son of Isaac Thomas Gatlin and married
first to Josie Merrell.

The old Isaac Gatlin Home place on Old School House Road –
Picture was made a few years ago when the property sold to David Walker.

Union Hill Baptist Church

U Nion Hill Baptist Church is no doubt the oldest Baptist Church in the area having been organized in 1832. From 1832 to 1852, the congregation met in the old Smyrna school house which was still being used as a school. The school was located at the bottom of George Smith Hill (Spook Hollow) at the old Orval Currin home place. In the early days church met just once each month.[38]

The first church building was erected across the road from the George Smith home at the top of the hill which is now known as Ardmore Ridge Road. The deed is dated May 10, 1852. Trustees at the time were Henry K. Lewter, father of deceased Ardmore resident, Dewey Lewter, and Andrew Smith father of now deceased Sherman Smith who married Lora Merrell. The church stood in this location for 57 years.

Early records have been lost, but in addition to the Smiths, and Lewters, there were Merrells, Whitts, Currins, and Whites who lived in the area and attended Union Hill Church.

In 1908 the church was moved to its present site to accommodate parishioners. The land was purchased from Mr. and Mrs. T. L. Williams.

Although everyone takes electricity for granted now, at that time almost all churches were lit by kerosene or gas lamps.

Over the years, the church has been remodeled. In the early 1960's, new Sunday school rooms, bathrooms and a kitchen were added. In 1979, a major remodeling project was undertaken when the bapistry, carpet, central air and heat were installed. A fellowship hall was added and more class rooms were built. Members helped with this project, but the major portion of the work was done by Herman Bailey and Buddy Whitt.

The first parsonage was built by George Smith and his son, Malcolm Smith. It was destroyed by fire, and part of the old Smyrna

---

[38] Union Hill Baptist Church History by Laurene Schrimsher

School was moved across the road from the church and remodeled to use as a home for the pastor. The house was remodeled several times over the years, and in June 1995 it was sold and moved to make room for a new parsonage to be built.

The earliest recorded list of church pastors begins in 1923 when Bro. Yeager served the congregation. In 1925 L. A. Hatfield was pastor. That year the church had 87 members on the roll in Sunday school.

In 1928, Rev. Allen Steelman of Harvest, AL was called as pastor to the church. One hundred and two were on roll as members with 75 in Sunday school. Superintendent was Matt Lewter. Minutes for several years are unavailable, but in 1932, L. A. Hatfield was once again pastor and membership had grown to 126. Church clerk for that year was Lewis H. Merrell. Recorded deaths for that year included Rev. J. T. Thompson, Jim Wilson and Mrs. Loda White
.

In 1934, Nathan Merrell was listed as executive board member and Mabron Lewter was church clerk. The church membership had grown to 154 and the pastor's salary was $250.

L. M. Mayer of Minor Hill, TN was pastor of the church in 1936, and Matt Lewter was executive board member. Sunday school superintendent was Cletis Stevenson. Membership was 138. There was one death that year, Mrs. Henry Lewter whose death was recorded in 1936.

Edward Lee served the congregation as pastor from 1938 to 1940. In 1939 the Sunday school superintendent was Logan Smith. Robert Smith was the clerk. One death was recorded that year, that of Mrs. Tishie Smith.

In 1942 when George Brown was pastor, there were 145 members. Mabron Lewter was superintendent and Mrs. Carl Ussery was clerk. Deaths that year included B. W. White, Mrs. Josie Gatlin (wife of Isaac Gatlin) and Matt Lewter, who was a deacon.

The war years found Union Hill Church affected as were all the churches in the area. In 1943 several from the church were drafted or volunteered for the Army. These included Erskin Brown, James Cross, Fred Stevenson, Robert Smith, Lawrence Smith, and Raymond Woodard. G. C. Morris was pastor from 1943-44 and there were 155 members.

In 1945 M. H. Willingham was called as pastor to the church and left in 1946. Membership at the time was 142 with 56 attending Sunday school. D. B. Brooker was then ordained as minister at a salary of $288.71. One death was recorded in 1946, that of Mrs. A. M. Lewter.

Next to serve as pastor was J. C. Wilbanks. The church clerk was Mrs. Carl Ussery with Milton Maddox as superintendent. Pastor's salary had increased to $764.

G. C. Smith was called as pastor in 1948 to serve 146 members. Church property was valued at $3,500. Deaths that year included Mrs. Nona Ross Lewter Shelton, Deacon George Smith, and Edward S. Lewter. Rev. Smith continued to serve though 1949 with membership at 150. There were several deaths recorded that year: Mrs. Jennie Brown Lewter, Mrs. Corinne Lewter Ussery, Mrs. Mary Lewter Van Hoozer and Mrs. Margaret Gatlin Merrell.

Pastor F. E. Durham served the congregation from 1950 through 1953. In 1950 Marion Lewter was church clerk and L. T. Shannon was superintendent. There were 150 members. Three deaths were recorded 1in 1950: Mrs. B. W. Whitt, Mahlon Watson and G. B. Brown.

Giles County's abstract of deeds shows entries for some of the people who settled in the area north of where Union Hill Church stands. Entry 64 shows John Merrell purchasing 24.5 acres on the headwaters of the main fork of Sinking Creek on Elk River. He was the older brother of Garrett Merrell. This occurred June 29, 1824. The land was on the north boundary of Andrew Merrell, John Vance, and William Thompson. A Pleasant Merrell was also listed.

Elkmont Springs [39]

"It was a lively, thriving community around the turn of the century. Wealthy folks from the surrounding area traveled to Elkmont Springs, TN, each summer just to drink the water, which was thought to have curative powers, and to relax. They also came to bathe in the water and dance to lively music on the dance floor. But time has taken its toll on Elkmont Springs, and the village no longer exists.

---

[39] Article from Your Community Shopper, March 1992, by Loretta Ekis

Faces and Places of Yesterday

"Before Ardmore was a reality, Elkmont Springs was in its heyday. Two stores, one of which was owned by Jim Woodard, a blacksmith shop, hotel, dance hall and school were located in the village Ardmore's own Dr. Walter Johnson, now deceased, attended school here as did other youngsters of his day.

"The hotel with its mineral water was a big drawing card. According to a history by Odie Jones, an area resident now deceased; the hotel may have been one of the first in the area to automate its water supply system. Jones says, "There was a mineral spring down the hill just west of the hotel. They ran a stout wire from the hotel overhead down the hill to the spring and would let a bucket slide down the hill to the spring's water spout. When the bucket was filled, they would wind it back up the hill to the hotel." Must have saved a lot of hill climbing in that day.

"Another draw was the dance hall. Folks gathered at the old dance hall until it was hit by a tornado in 1936 and destroyed. According to William Broadway, a former resident of Ardmore, now deceased, the tornado hit Elkmont Springs that year destroying the dance hall and several houses. Elkmont Springs never recovered.

"Before the fatal storm, however, folks traveled to the hotel from all over. In the August 8, 1918 edition of the Democrat in Athens, AL, forty-five people from Athens went to a ball at Elkmont Springs. A notice in the June 6, 1918 paper stated that Miss Ola Mingea had rented Elkmont Springs for the coming season. The property was then owned by Ragsdale Realty.

"At the turn of the century, phone service was not available either in the village located in the SE corner of Giles County. Mail service was available, but post offices were either in stores or private homes. Folks back then didn't correspond very often, and there was no junk mail overflowing mailboxes as it does today. People still traveled by horse and buggy or wagon. Women still wore long, serviceable dresses with skirts that dragged the floor, and children were taught to be seen but not heard.

"To the younger generation, the village might never have existed, but a few of the older generation can remember the Elkmont Springs Resort, and to those few, it is a memory they cherish. How wonderful if

102

those memories could be imprinted, such as a photograph, to be savored by future generations.

"Mr. Odie Jones stated in his book, "As I Remember it," only three houses was between my home near Piney Grove Church and Elkmont Springs, TN, four miles northwest and is now the northwest side of Ardmore. But Ardmore was not there then." Imagine that if you can.

The earliest record discovered concerning the springs was November 1857. A notice appeared that stated on Tuesday, Dec. 1 at the residence of Samuel D. White, deceased, an auction would be held. The property known as Price's Springs, but had lately been known as White's Springs would be sold. The White's children were Thomas W. White, Virginia Ann Eddins, and Edward F. White.[40]

Elkmont Springs School and other land deeds

Elkmont Springs School was established in 1886 when W. S. Ezell Deeded ½ acre of land for the school. S. A. Gorden and W. J. McNeeley served as directors for the school. The land was to be used for the school, but it would revert back to Ezell should it be abandoned or the school ceased to exist. The date of the deed was July 12, 1886.

Yet another entry shows John Austin recorded 94 acres on the waters of Sinking Creek. His property was on the west side of Isaac Major, William Richardson, Samuel Jordon, John Vance, Sarah Vance and the county line. Date was June 29, 1824. Also mentioned was Joseph Calvert.

---

[40] Giles Free Press May 12, 1994

Maggie Merrell and Maude Coffman
With unknown child

Celebrating Dealie Merrell's 84th Birthday at Granny's Kitchen
L to R, Marge McConnell, Ginger Retka, Dealie Merrell,
and Beverly Browning with Mike Browning in back.

Saints and Sinners of Yesterday

As is usually the case, history is recorded both formally and informally. The following entries have been recorded in family histories, newspapers, official documents, and from the memories of some who are still living. Sometimes the events are good, sometimes they aren't as flattering, but such is history. That is why this section is titled "Saints and Sinners of Yesterday." Sometimes people are saints and sometimes sinners, but we are all human, and sometimes that means we're a little of both at the same time. This section will give you some idea of what happened in the past, but nothing here is intended to be judgmental or reflect poorly on the people of that day. It's all history, and rewriting history isn't an option.

Since the sinners usually capture the headlines, we'll start off this section with one who did in his day – Will Baird.[41]

Will Baird was born in Wilson County, TN and reared in Davidson County, TN, but he had ties to Lincoln County – cousins. He came to Lincoln County and married his cousin, Mary Roper, 16, daughter of G. T. Roper of Roperton, near Blanche.

Mr. Roper was a very prosperous man and accumulated considerable property – reputed to be the wealthiest man in the neighborhood. It is reported that Baird had dissipated the portion of his wife's estate on which he could lay hands and insisted upon her conveying to him her landed interests.

The story goes that he took his wife on Friday, Dec. 1, 1905, to Fayetteville for dinner at the Spon Hotel. He is said to have been attentive to her, but that she ate little. On the way home that evening about dust she was shot and killed while seated in the buggy near Blanche.

The bullet entered the right temple and her face was powder burned showing that the pistol was within a few inches of her face when fired. Baird rode with the dead body of his wife about five miles, passing

---

[41] This story was researched by Kenneth Smith – from articles in the Fayetteville Observer and court documents.

several residences, but didn't tell of it until he reached the home of a relative. It was reported that he passed 21 houses and a man in the road that had a lighted lantern.[42]

Baird seemed anxious to have the body buried on Saturday, but the interment was delayed by the neighbors until an inquest was conducted by Esq. F. R. Mitchell. The verdict of the jury followed.

Jury Verdict - The jurors, under oath, came to the conclusion on Dec. 2, 1905, that Mrs. Baird came to her death by a pistol shot by the hand of her husband, C. W. Baird, and that it was feloniously done. The jurors were: A. D. Gatlin, Y. N. Gatlin, B. F. Whitt, E. B. Bolin, L. C. Mitchell, F. R. Wallace, Nathan Smith, with F. R. Mitchell, J.P.

Baird claimed that he was waylaid and his wife shot by an unknown assassin – one man held his mule by the bit and his wife was shot by a man standing by the buggy as she leaned forward in order to see past him, but the bullet had entered the temple next to him and not in the face. The skin was also badly discolored by the powder.

The Bairds were parents of two girls, aged 12 and 8 years. They had also buried an infant in the Roper Cemetery who was born and died on January 2, 1896.

Baird's story was not believed, and the circumstantial evidence, pointed to his guilt. Sheriff Taylor arrested him on Sunday and placed him in the Lincoln County jail.

Hearing held – On Thursday of the following week, a hearing was held before W. N. Whitaker, Esq. Baird's lawyers were Estill & Newman, S. C. Tigert and J. J. Lynch. The prosecution called witnesses, and the defendant waved further examination and was committed to jail. It was reported that Baird didn't seem to fully appreciate the seriousness of the charges against him and often laughed when something laughable was said. The case against him was not as strong as expected, it was reported at the time, but that it was possible they simply wanted to prove the commission of the crime, which was all that was necessary in the

---

[42] The case was mentioned as late as 2013 in an article entitled "The Slayer Statute" by Donald Paine, Tennessee Bar Association.

magistrate court. The case against Baird, charged with murder of his wife, was set for Wednesday, Dec. 21. Judge Higgins presided over the trial.

The trial of C. W. Baird began on Wednesday, Dec. 21, 1905. By Friday, the testimony ended, and the case went to the jury on Monday afternoon. Members of the jury were: C. A. Bedwell, J. A. Stubblefield, J. A. Taylor, J. N. Cole, J. C. Ellis, J. E. Kent, G. M. Morgan, E. E. Jordan, W. T. Rudd, C. M. Finley, Rufus Bryant and W. R. Loyd.

Baird took the witness stand on Friday before the case went to the jury and claimed that his wife was shot by robbers. The tale he told did not seem plausible, but it is said he was a good witness for himself. In the cross examination, however, he became somewhat tangled and did not to the satisfaction of many of the hearers, explain his passing 24 houses after the fatal shot to ask for assistance.

It was said that the judge gave the accused every chance to establish his innocence, and there was no error committed by him on which an appeal could be based. Both sides conducted their case with consummate skill, it was noted, and every inch of ground was covered.

On Tuesday morning, the jury had a verdict. The circumstantial evidence was enough to establish Baird's guilt, and the jury found him guilty as charged. Application was made for a new trial and heard on Wednesday morning. Judge Higgins overruled the request saying among other things, that he was either guilty or innocent, there was no mitigation. The prisoner was told to stand and asked if there was any reason the sentence of death should not be pronounced upon him. He replied, "I must say that I am innocent." Judge Higgins then passed the death sentence finding Friday, April 13, as the day of execution. Baird reportedly received the sentence without tremor or emotion.

After the mother's death, the Baird children were cared for by Mrs. W. T. Beddingfield. Baird attempted to gain custody of them so that he might send them to live with his sister, Mrs. John Bond, of Uniontown, Kentucky. A decision was delayed for 45 days. The court later gave Mrs. Beddingfield custody of the children.

The Baird land was sold for $2,350 with $500 going to the children and the remainder going to settle accounts.

Faces and Places of Yesterday

Baird Executed – Baird's case was appealed to the Supreme Court whose long writing outlined the case and cited Baird's statements and showed the improbability of vermilion. (sic)…(*editor's note: unsure of the exact meaning of this word.*) In the end, the court said the guilt of the prisoner was clearly shown and the judgment of the lower court was upheld.

One petition to Gov. Patterson was made by George H. Newman asking that the sentence be commuted to life in prison. The governor granted a second respite and named May 24 as the date of execution.

His children were taken to see him, and he told them that even though they had been taught that he murdered their mother that he did not, and that he would die innocent of the crime. Baird continued to claim he was innocent until his death.

On the day of execution, after having breakfast, Baird was taken to the platform. Sheriff Taylor told Baird, "William you have been a good prisoner; giving us no trouble, and we appreciate it. Now I'm going to give you a little time to talk." Baird stepped out on the trap and said, "Mr. Taylor has made me a good jailor, and has been kind to me, and I appreciate it. I have a statement in my pocket. That is all I have to say."

Doctor Goodner besought Baird to confess if guilty saying, "Baird, in a few moments you will be in eternity and, if you are guilty, tell it. If you expect to meet your God, don't die with a lie on your lips." J. A. Formwalt, at this time urged Baird to confess saying, "Bill, if you did it, let it come." In a cool and collected manner, Baird responded firmly, "Gentlemen, you have heard what I said."

The trap was sprung at 5:08 a.m., May 24, 1907. The body was taken to Formwalt & Son's undertaking establishment where it was embalmed and prepared for burial.

Baird asked to buried beside his wife and daughter, but this request was met with strenuous objects and the body was buried in Leatherwood Cemetery in the SW portion of the county. At least, that is the official story of the burial. Was Baird guilty of killing his own wife? The state said yes, and many believed he was. In the end only Baird and God knows for certain.

Ardmore Bank Robbery – On Wednesday morning, January 5, 1950, the Bank of Ardmore was robbed of $1,734.[43]

J. Tully Brown, cashier, was in the bank when two Athens men, later identified as W. C. (Chicken) Downs, 27, and Joe Smith, 41, entered the bank. They ordered Brown and three others into the vault where they were forced to kneel. It was believed a third and possibly a fourth man waited in a car.

The two bandits, described as youthful in appearance, placed handkerchiefs over their faces and entered the bank. Drawing a pistol, one of them said, "This is a holdup." One stood guard while the other took money from inside the vault.

They locked the employees in the vault and left. On the way out, they took some money from a drawer, but overlooked another drawer containing $2,200. All told, they managed to get less than $2,000, fleeing in an automobile.

The vault was unlocked and the employees freed shortly after the bandits fled. The employees were John T. Brown, his wife, a clerk, Issac Gatlin, assistant cashier, and Hubert Roper.

The get-away car was described as a black Ford Coupe with a Limestone County tag, 44C-816. Limestone County Sheriff John G. Sandlin said the license was listed in the name of Murray Yarbrough, Belle Mina School, 15 miles from Athens. The sheriff added that he believed the car had been stolen from Hillary Nash in Athens that morning.

The bandits, it was believed, transferred to a black Packard sedan, which was seen parked several miles north of Ardmore, in Giles County. Officer from Limestone County, Lincoln and Giles Counties in Tennessee and the FBI and Tennessee Highway Patrol joined in the investigation.

Now that was the official report in a newspaper. Following is the real story as reported by Mrs. Clyde Franklin:

---

[43] Athens Newspaper story, Thursday, January 5, 1950

Faces and Places of Yesterday

Cash Point News – Thursday, January 12, 1950[44] – "Now that the excitement of the Ardmore Bank Robbery has died down, I'll tell you what actually happened. Hubert Roper says it was the most harrowing experience since the day he was forced to use his new fire extinguisher when his automobile caught fire. He declares that gun looked a yard long when the bandit pointed it at him and said, 'Stick 'em up.'

"Mrs. Brown thought of that beautiful ring Mr. Brown gave her at Christmas, took it off, and put it in her mouth. What if she had hiccupped? In a way the robbery was like an old fashioned prayer meeting. 'They all knelt there' at the bandits' command.

"Isaac Gatlin was so scared his knees beat out a tune like, 'Mule Train.'

"Just outside the bank stood a group of Cash Pointers, Floyd Smith, Malc Helums, and Sherman Bolin, discussing cotton acreage cuts in Lincoln County. The subject was so hot they failed to see the robbers enter the bank. Then the burglar alarm sounded. Sherman narrowly escaped injury. The bandits fleeing with cash in one hand, gun in the other almost tripped over him, and Sherman still so upset at what was happening mistook the burglar alarm for the fire alarm and ran out into the street to see Ardmore's new fire truck if it went by, and that was when the robbers almost backed over him in their getaway.

"Stunned beyond words, Floyd motioned to Sherman and they rushed in the bank to find Mr. Brown had freed the four employees from the vault. A quick count showed $1,734 missing. Police were notified and the search started.

"All suspects were brought in and Sherman and Floyd were asked to identify them, and after a few days' work with the FBI and others, their names (*editor's note…the names of Floyd and Sherman*) didn't even get in the paper. All this happened about 10 a.m. Tuesday morning and by Thursday noon, the bandits were captured and the money recovered.

---

[44] Cash Point News, January 12, 1950, Mrs. Clyde Franklin Reporter

"Sherman went home to his wife and kids and Floyd went back to the job of horse swappin' with the excitement of detective work only a memory."

One must admit that straight reporting is sometimes less fun than a columnist's writings, as were many of Mary Lou Franklin's in the 1950s.

Mitt Henderson, 53, Accidentally Killed[45] - "Mr. Mitt Henderson, aged 53 years, a prominent farmer of the Cash Point community, was killed by the explosion of five sticks of dynamite last Monday morning.

"Mr. Henderson had started out to some blasting on his farm and was carrying the dynamite in a shoebox. On crossing a fence, he accidentally dropped the box and the dynamite exploded. He lived about ten hours after the accident.

"The funeral services were conducted at Blanche by Rev. W. J. Malone of Hazel Green, Ala. Burial took place in Blanche Cemetery.

"Mr. Henderson is survived by his wife, who was before her marriage, Miss Cora Maddox, of Blanche and the following children: Virginia, Thelma, Wayne, Jean, Clen and Harold."

Death of R. B. Hayes[46] - Letter to the editor: "Mr. Editor – I wish to inform your readers (if you will not consider me presuming) something concerning the late R. B. Hayes (col) better known by the name of Crowie. He was daily the unfavored guest of about 60 or 70 persons. He departed this life in a rather mysterious way – said to be murdered. The civil rights bill does not guarantee to the colored the right of attending public school with the whites. Hence the trouble and perhaps owning to this R. B. met his fate, as he did it unwantonly. The writer of this piece can compare it to nothing but a lad who had a favorite pup he wished to train up for a bear dog. Therefore, he asked the old man to robe himself in a bear skin. He accordingly did so; when all was ready the boy hissed the pup on where he immediately downed the old man. The boy hissed, the old man hollered.

---

[45] Lincoln County News, January 8, 1931
[46] Fayetteville Observer, August 23, 1877, Cash Point, TN

"R. B. being dead of course hurts his friends, but it is the making of the school. Different parties are charged with the murder and other as accessory to it. A recent investigation instead of throwing light on the subject seems to obscure it. A jury of inquest decided that perhaps he was killed after he was dead, as it was proven that he was seen alive after he was dead." *(Editor's note: I only hope that when the letter ran in the paper that everyone understood the story because in this later day...it is not clear at all what the school had to do with the bearskin impersonator, or etc. That story should have never been printed in 1877, but it is so unusual it is being reprinted here.)*

Horse Thieves Captured – Even without many law enforcement personnel in 1880 and no computers or phones, thieves didn't always get away with stealing horses. The following was reported on May 13, 1880.[47]

Sol and Alec Bledsoe, of Giles County, were captured in Wayne County arrested and jailed in Pulaski in 1880. They had stolen three horses that were in their possession when captured. Apparently, there were others stealing as well.

Alec and Sol Bledsoe, had stolen horses from Alabama, and the owners appeared at the trial and paid $75 reward offered for their arrest. When this was done, the prosecution was abandoned and their release ordered. As soon as the handcuffs were removed, the Alabama men took the prisoners in charge and immediately re-ironed them. Their authority for this proceeding was demanded by Mr. Taliaferro, attorney for the Bledsoe's, but they declined to exhibit either warrant or requisition. They stated, however, that if it became necessary, they were prepared to show that they were authorized to make the arrest. The matter was not pressed and the prisoners were mounted on a mule and carried to Athens, Alabama for trial.

A different article in the same issue of the Citizen shows that Sheriff Arrowsmith, who arrested the two Bledsoe's, was suffering from a thumb that was badly mutilated by the teeth of the ruffian, Bledsoe.

---

[47] Pulaski Citizen, May 13, 1880

In a somewhat related incident, the following was reported: For several weeks, the neighborhood adjacent to Cash Point, in the SW part of Giles County and Elkton, had been "agitated and indignant at the depredations of horse thieves who plied their nocturnal avocation with assiduity. Two mules were stolen from David Neal, 8 miles south of Pulaski. They were tracked to Elkton and found tied in the bushes. A man named Fowler, believed to be an accomplice, asserted that E. I. Brownlow admitted that he stole the mules from the stables while Eddins watched.

They were arrested, taken to Elkton, arraigned and required to give bond of $1,000 and to appear at the next Giles County Circuit Court. In default, Brownlow went to jail; Eddins paid the sheriff $500 in cash, gave security for the remainder, and then "went west."

It seems the Bledsoe's had more woes than those mentioned above. Alexander Bledsoe served in time in Alabama, and then apparently left the area. Sol who went west, actually ended up in Texas where he was killed by a train fireman in a shootout.

Harvey M. Bledsoe – was born 26 February 1813 in Tennessee and died February 19, 1877.[48] He was buried in the Bledsoe Cemetery in Lincoln County.

A local newspaper article ran the following story on Oct. 21, 1869:[49] "On Sunday, 10th inst., about 10 o'clock at night, Thomas (Dutch) Baugh was shot and killed by an unknown party about 4 miles west of Pleasant Plains. His body was riddled with buckshot from his heart up. Pistols were also fired, and a stray ball from one struck Braxton Neil's home, slightly wounding Mrs. Neil. The Nashville Banner has a statement of the cause of difficulty, which we are told, is substantially correct.

"We copy: About ten days ago Holloway and Baugh fired upon an old man named Bledsoe in his own house. He returned the fire and they retreated. Their object was probably to revenge themselves on his sons, whom they suspected had whipped them. After Bledsoe fired upon (them), Baugh and Holloway met one of his sons and drew pistols on him and made him get on his knees and beg for his life. Sunday night last, the two

---

[48] Bledsoe Family Bible
[49] The Fayetteville Observer

were in the neighborhood of the Bledsoe's. They are supposed to have been intoxicated. They were making threats against Bledsoe and sons. While riding along the road they were fired upon in an ambush. Baugh was killed and Holloway's horse shot out from under him. Holloway made his escape."

About a month later, H. M. Bledsoe answered these charges with the following: [50] "Since myself and others were legally acquitted on the charge of lying in wait, and murdering one Thomas Baugh, before the Magistrate's Court, last week, I have been informed that reports were rife in the country that our discharge was procured by a compromise between myself and the prosecutor. And as the charge of said murder was maliciously and falsely coupled with our names, through some of the journals of the state – from erroneous information given said journals by parties unknown to us, I deem it but prudent, and justice to myself and those arraigned with me, to procure from the committing magistrates, before whom the case was heard, the following statement of facts, over their signatures, and present the same to the public for one purpose only, to wit – That our friends may know our true status in the matter. Signed H. M. Bledsoe.

A statement dated November 18, 1869, signed by W. O. Price, J.P. was presented showing that H. M. Bledsoe, Alex Bledsoe, Solomon Bledsoe, Buck Bledsoe (son of Stephen) and Buck Bledsoe (son of James) were not charged in the death of Thomas Baugh because of no evidence of guilt. Apparently, this cleared the matter though gossip is hard to stop.

Lewis Jefferson Bledsoe – A death notice from the Fayetteville Observer on July 26, 1923 shows that L. J. Bledsoe, son of Harvey M., died at the age of 83 years, 4 months and 2 days at his home in Fayetteville on July 19, 1923. Mr. Bledsoe had served as a soldier in the Confederate Army. He was a member of the missionary Baptist church. He is buried at Blanche Cemetery. He was married to Francis Elizabeth Carter and had the following children: Wallace T., Lewis J. Jr., James H. Bledsoe, MD., and Mary Elizabeth "Mollie"Bledsoe.

---

[50] The information is shows as on a card, dated Nov. 18, 1869

Blanche [51] - "There was considerable excitement raised near Cash Point some four miles from this place, on last Saturday night. While on their way from church at that place, Bailer Leatherwood shot and fatally wounded W. W. (Bill) Roper. This grew out of an old grudge. Two shots were fired, the first taking effect in the stomach. The ball has not been located. Roper walked more than 100 yards after being shot and was then carried home. They were four feet apart when the shooting was done. Both are under age and of respectable families. The former is the son of Mrs. Fannie Leatherwood, and the latter the son of James T. Roper. Leatherwood made his escape."

This columnist went on to write that the Rev. H. B. Blakely of South Carolina, who supplied the A.R.P. pulpit at this place, a few summers ago, is expected to begin a meeting at this place on Friday night before the second Sabbath of July. We hope all who can will hear him.

Mrs. Cordie Sloan is spending a few days with her sister, Mrs. Ella Moore, near Molino.

Mrs. Blanche Toney of Madison Cross Roads, was visiting her father, Mr. J. R. Rawls, not many days ago.

It is interesting that in one paragraph Plow boy was reporting a murder and in the next reporting that an out of state preacher would be holding a meeting. Saints and sinners, indeed!

Blanche – article by Plow Boy[52] - "Mr. Archie Gatlin of Cash Point, met with a rather sad accident a few days ago while trying to burst a log with powder. After boring a hole and placing in his powder and pin, he was sitting on the log trying to light the fuse. Thinking it had gone out, he was setting another when the pin blew out, tearing off his thumb and lacerating one hand badly. It also took off most of an ear and threw splinters in his eye. He has been suffering a good deal. The wounds were dressed by Dr. L. S. Freeman.

Robinson Children – Two of the children of W. B. Robinson happened to have a serious and painful accident not many days ago, but not

---

[51] Fayetteville Observe, June 18, 1892 (Plow Boy article)
[52] Fayetteville Observer, March 19, 1896

on the same day. A little son who was chopping stove wood came near severing three of his toes with the axe. It bled severely before a physician could reach him. Last week an older son, Jimmie, was helping his father roll a loaded wagon backward under the barn shelter, when he slipped and started to fall and the wagon bed caught his jaw between it and some other object, breaking his jawbone. He is doing as well as could be expected at this time.[53]

Fatal Accident at Cash Point[54] – "At Cash Point last Friday morning about 9 o'clock Esq. A. D. Gatlin while at work at a cotton gin had his arm caught and the flesh was stripped off to the elbow. He lived until 4 o'clock that afternoon when death mercifully relieved his sufferings. He was a splendid citizen and one of the most influential men of that neighborhood. He was a member of the Missionary Baptist Church and took an active interest in every movement intended for the betterment of the community. Such a man is a blessing to the locality in which he lives and his death is a public calamity. The funeral service was attended by the largest gathering ever assembled at a similar occasion in that neighborhood, the people thus attesting to the regard for him and sorrow at his death. The burial was by the Woodmen of the World, of which fraternity he was a member, after services by Rev. W. J. Malone. Mr. Gatlin was 46 years, 6 months and 17 days old and is survived by his wife and seven children."

Struck by Lightning – "At noon last Friday, the large barn at Cash Point belonging to Mr. Sim Smith was struck by lightning and burned. It was a very large structure and the loss is conservatively estimated at $2,000, on which there was insurance for $750 in the Continental. At the time of the putting up of the lightning rod, the company guaranteed against lightning for five years and the guaranty had run up only a few months ago. Word of the accident was telephoned around and by 1 o'clock there were seventy men in the lot who got out about thirty barrels of corn, which they shucked and put in another barn. About fifty barrels of corn with other feedstuff was lost."[55] (*Editor's note – Not certain that phones were actually available in Cash Point at this time.*)

---

[53] Fayetteville Observer, May 4, 1899
[54] Fayetteville Observer, March 29, 1917
[55] Fayetteville Observer, March 29, 1917

A Still Captured – "Last Friday Sheriff Newman and Joe L. Caughran found a still near Cash Point. The outfit had been dismantled and concealed but sleuths of the law were on a hot trail and kept searching until they found it." [56] No indication as to where it was found.

Electricity Comes to Lincoln County – Ardmore and Fayetteville and communities in between, Camargo, Molino, Blanche, Elora, Kelso, Coldwater, McBurg, Boonshill, Lincoln, Flintville, Bellville, Howell Hill, Taft, Cyruston, Cash Point, Bellview, Frankewing, Mimosa, Kirkland, Liberty, Brighton, Yukon, Pear City and Egan, all were excited when on Oct. 1, 1935, the Tennessee Valley Authority turned on electricity in these rural areas.

Invitations were sent to Mrs. Franklin D. Roosevelt, Gov. Hill McAlister, and Gov. Bill Graves of Alabama, Senators Kenneth D. McKellar and Nathan L. Bachman, Congressman J. Ridley Mitchell and the entire congressional delegation of Tennessee.

Mary Sloan, the 10-year-old daughter of the late Lawrence Sloan of Taft, Tenn. Was selected to throw the switch.

J. D. Hamilton's Death[57] - "As a result of an automobile accident, J. D. Hamilton Jr., 19, farmer of the Cash Point Community, died Thursday night, Oct. 8, at the Lincoln County Hospital. He sustained a broken arm and internal injuries when the car in which he was riding crashed into a bridge three miles from Cash Pont, forcing an iron railing into the car side, pinning him there.

Two other occupants, John Elliot, 20 and Doc Smith, were thrown on the bridge and knocked unconscious. Regaining their senses, they called Elgie Hopwood, who was nearby, and he assisted in freeing Hamilton and brought him to the hospital.

The three youths had been visiting friends and were returning home when the accident occurred.

---

[56] Fayetteville Observer, August 17, 1922
[57] Fayetteville Observer, Oct. 15, 1936

Funeral service was conducted Friday afternoon at the Baptist Church at Cash Point by Rev. B. E. Franklin of Huntsville and Rev. G. C. Morris of Blanche. Burial was in the Blanche Cemetery. He was survived by his parents, James (Jim) and Ethel Ferguson Hamilton and his sister, Mrs. Clyde Franklin. He was preceded in death by a sister Jenny Pearl Hamilton.

Pitts and Odell Merrell - Odell later married Bedford Whitt and Pitts married Archie K. Arnett. Photo made at the home of James Franklin Merrell.

Faces and Places of Yesterday

The items in this section of the book were taken from various sources and simply show what was happening in the area many years ago. Life was so much simpler then, and people really were good neighbors!

Mrs. Lillie Barnett – "If you've ever moved, you know that you always run across something that you hadn't seen since the last move. Well, Mrs. Lillie Barnett has some false teeth that get in her way at moving time that she would gladly swap for a lawn mower."[58]

Kelly's Creek News[59]– Letter to the Observer in 1884 – "As there has been nothing written from this vicinity lately, we proceed to give you a few items for publication.

"There is a little sickness in the neighborhood. Our farmers are moving briskly over the furrowed fields, straining every nerve to finish the planting of corn. Wheat that was sown very early looks fine and promises a good yield, but that which was sown late last fall does not appear favorable to a good yield.

"Mr. Milton Smith, one of our best citizens, is making preparations for building to build for his comfort an elegant dwelling. The Jones Brothers, excellent carpenters, have contracted to do the work.

"We are credibly informed that the Baptist brethren are making the necessary preparations to rear a church – a building which is badly needed. It will be constructed on the modern style. We trust there will be little difficulty in consummating the movement. Our devoted pastor, Mr. Hilliard, made a thrilling talk on the subject of the old church last Sunday with marked effect.

"Mr. Thomas F. Towry, who took charge of the school at Cash Point last December, will close out his school there next Friday and considering the fact that he had to introduce the normal methods of educating from the very outset, his classes have made a wonderful progress. He will take charge of Kelly's Creek school again the coming summer.

---

[58] Cash Point News, Thursday, January 20, 1944, Mrs. Clyde Franklin, Reporter
[59] Fayetteville Observer, April 19, 1884

"Some of our young men (Mr. P. L. Hill in particular) were becoming sorely distress, as leap year is rapidly passing away, and the girls are so extremely slow in making the long hoped for proposals. Don't fret boys, your time will come by and by."

An announcement was received February 25, 1886 that postmasters were announced by telegraph from Washington. They were W. A. Franklin, Cash Point and S. E. Noblett, County Line.

William Carroll McRee – He was born Jan. 21, 1826 in Lincoln County about 1 mile from Boonshill. He lived there until he was 10 years old then moved with his family to another farm until 1941 when his father died and his mother married Thomas McAfee. He continued to live with them until 1846 when he married. He married Barshaba Paysinger who was born April 12, 1826.

McRee moved to the south side of the Elk River and stayed there for a while, then moved back to Kelly's Creek in 1858. He stayed there until Dec. 24, 1873 then moved to Shoal Creek in Giles County where he bought 100 acres from Granville H. Gatlin. In the fall of 1861, he entered the army and fought for the South, but was wounded on Dec. 29, 1862, and went home. Barshaba died on Feb. 25, 1893. They had the following children: William Carroll McRee born March 1847 married Pricilla Gatlin, Rhody Angeline McRee born Oct. 1849 married John Wesley McAfee, James Carson McRee born Sept. 1851 married Winney Caroline Gatlin, David Wilson McRee, born Feb. 1856, John Henderson McRee born Sept. 1858 married Dicey Oldent, and George Alexander Isaac McRee born Sept. 1865 married M. E. Ashford and Barshaba Syntha McRee married Nimrod Golden Gatlin son of Isaac Gatlin. The elder William Carroll McRee died July 15, 1905.[60]

William Carroll McRee Sr., was the son of James McRee who was born Oct. 1779 and married Elizabeth Fain in 1814. James died in 1841, James was the son of John McRee and his mother was Ruth Alexander. The elder McRee's are buried in Charlotte, NC.

[60] William Carroll McRee Bible

Cash Point Post Office – In January 1877 a new post office was established about 4 miles west of Blanche. This post office was established years before Ardmore was settled, an interesting fact that no one would guess today.[61] The following letter to the editor appeared on April 19, 1877 in the Observer:

"Editor Observer – If it would not be an imposition on my part, I desire to inform your readers about our newly established post office, Cash Point – as I am aware of the fact that many of the readers of the Observer do not know that there is such a place in existence as Cash Point.

"Some persons recently of Kelso Station, hearing of Cash Point, conceived the idea that it was situated between the two Fayetteville Banks, at a saloon there. But to those parties at Kelso, I would say, not much saloon. The place we have reference to is about twenty-three miles south west of Fayetteville, on Fort Hampton Road, vulgarly known as the Old State Line Road. The population of this place is not very extensive. The place belongs primarily to John W. Gatlin, Esq. – a man who has energy enough to move a mountain if necessary.

"We have a good school in this place, where our young are making preparations for future usefulness. The people of the vicinity are an industrious, economical people, and are farming this season as with a pre-determination to do something. They raise more cotton in this portion of the county than any other. (Signed) Respectfully, J."

Cash Point Baptist Church's 100th Anniversary – the historical committee consisted of: Kathleen Henderson, Cass Smith, Margaret Smith, Houston Franklin, Harold and Don Owen, Marion Hicks and Calvin and Peggy Holt.[62]

During the celebration, members brought in antiques to display which included shoe buttoners, cotton sacks, side saddles and quilts. There were also those who quilted, carved wood, washed clothes by hand in the old fashioned way, shelled corn and used treadle sewing machines.

---

[61] Fayetteville Observer, January 25, 1877
[62] Letter written by the Cash Point Historical Committee, undated

There were also exhibits to show the more simple way of life around the end of the 19th century. One song that stood out from all the rest was the song, "The Old Country Church." A book of church history was printed and made available by Buddy Mitchell.

Bryan Kennedy, son of Rev. Raymond Kennedy, visited and toured the church building and grounds. Bryan grew up in the old and new parsonage and lived in Cash Point from the time he was three until he was past 18 years of age.

Another visitor for the homecoming was Karen Malin, great-granddaughter of charter member Robert L. Gatlin. She and her family were visiting from Spring Hill, Tennessee.

A Memory of Ruby Smith Hopper, 1997 – "The church's first pastor was Rev. Con Smith." Ruby's father was William Franklin Smith who was born in 1875. His parents died when he was 12 years old and he lived with his uncle, Rev. Smith until he was 21.[63]

Ruby says her first memory of the church was when she was six years old. She was in the Card Class in Sunday school. Her teacher was a cousin, Mary Jane Holman. The class met in the old Amen Corner, a space where the men sat on Sunday morning.

"We were baptized in what is known as "Little Creek" on the TN-AL line – the Hopwood farm." Her family later moved and became members of Ardmore Baptist Church. Ruby was 11 years old when she was baptized in 1921.

Woodmen of the World Honor – Mrs. Essie Merrell, a member of Grove 6285, Fayetteville, a Cash Point resident, was presented a 50-year Woodmen membership pin by Field Rep. J. Everett Clark.[64] Mrs. Essie was the mother of Lucille Mitchell and Hazel Smith. Her picture was included in the June 1967 issue of the Woodmen magazine.

Mrs. Clyde Franklin – Mary Lou Franklin, home food supply chairman of the Cash Point Community Club, was selected as "Woman of

---

[63] Memories of Ruby Smith Hopper, 1997
[64] Woodmen of the World Magazine, June 1967

the Year" for Lincoln County in 1950. She won the honor over representatives from 20 other Home Demonstration Clubs in the county.[65] She was chosen from a field of 21 contestants, and presented with a vase of roses by Ann Russell, from Radio Station WSM in Nashville, guest speaker.

Henry Bayless – He was president of the Cash Point Community Club having been elected in 1948. He led the club during the period when the community was refurbishing, learning new crop methods and participating in the Chamber of Commerce contest.

Community Hayride – On Tuesday, August 21, 1952, the community held an old fashioned hayride. Their mode of transportation was modernized since instead of the horse-drawn steel-tired wagon, Doc Smith's tractor pulled a rubber-tired wagon overflowing with kids and adults alike.

A Slogan – Cash Point might have been one of the first places in the country to go green…at least by 1952 standards. Their motto was "Keeping Cash Point Green, keeps Cash Point Out of the Red."

Community News from 1952 – Doc Smith's house had burned on April 30, and when the work to rebuild began, more than 30 men volunteered to get logs cut and hauled for the framework. [66]

When Carl Cross was laid up in bed, his neighbors turned out to turn his crop land as he watched from his window. He said it was good insurance to live in Cash Point. Most felt the same way.

Another resident who needed assistance was Logan Smith who was hospitalized for a week or more. More than 60 people showed up and before the afternoon was half over, two bales of cotton was picked and ready for the gin.

M. A. Smith despite doctor's orders, insisted on planting a cotton patch, so friends went down to his seven acre field to gather in the cotton.

---

[65] Cash Point Community News, Nov. 1, 1952
[66] Cash Point Community News, 1952

Mr. Smith showed his appreciation by offering them generous refreshments.

Televisions began to spring up in the Cash Point Community in 1952. The E. C. Barnett, Hilt Tuck, and Buddy Campbell families along with Don Owen purchased new television sets. Could they have been watching wrestling on Saturday nights?

Cash Point Baptist Church – was thriving and doing well in 1952. The church had an enrollment of 185, a SS enrollment of 200 and a BTU enrollment of 98. Their budget for the year was a little more than $3,900.

Quilting Party – The ladies in the community gathered at the home of Hazel Smith and quilted three quilts for Mrs. Ola Hicklen who had been ailing. These quilting parties were a wonderful way to enjoy the company of neighbors while helping others.

Storm Victims Benefit – In March 1952, more than 50 women worked all day quilting for the Red Cross at the community center. Material for 14 quilts was donated by individuals. Eight quilts were completed that day and six more were scheduled for completion a few days later. The quilts were to be donated to storm victims through the Red Cross.

Mail Man Appreciation – The 75 families that made up the Cash Point Community wished to show their appreciation to Mr. Dee Boggs who had served as their mail man for years. On Christmas Eve, packages were left in the mail box for him, and as he pulled them from each box his smile grew bigger and he waved more cheerfully. Mr. Boggs came to the church the next Sunday to thank everyone for their generosity. "Not from the dollars and cents standpoint, but the sentiment behind it," he told the church. [67]

The Bobby Minor store at U-Take-It was being replaced with a new build in 1952 in order to provide more products.

---

[67] Community Shows Appreciation to Mailman, CP Community News, 1952

Prized Heifer – Tommy Ray Hargrove, a member of the Cash Point 4-H Club, was pleased in 1952 to have a Jersey heifer that took second prize at the Madison County Fair. Both Tommy and Rabon Bayless showed at the Petersburg Colt Show and both placed in the "blue group." They were also placed in the blue group at the Lincoln County fair and in the State Fair. Rabon went to Memphis and his animal ended up winning 3rd in the Tri-State Fair. Billy Brown won first place in the 4-H cotton exhibit at the county fair.

Businesses in Cash Point in 1952 that advertised in the Community News were: Arnolds Grocery, Joe Roper Grocery, Gray Brothers Gin, A. B. Magnusson General Merchandise and Gas, J. H. Elliott agent for V-C Fertilizer, and Minor's Grocery.

Mrs. Algie Stalcup – Marie Merrell Broadway well remembers her 2nd grade teacher who was Mrs. Stalcup. She also had Mrs. Mildred Twitty in 3rd grade at Cash Point Elementary. Marie would have started to school about 1930, so these two teachers would have been there at least in 1931-32 and 1932-33. As an added point of interest, Mrs. Mildred Twitty went to Blanche High School to teach and taught both of Marie's sisters, Loretta and Faye, between 1953 and 1961.

Jack Arnett's death – Mr. Odie Jones wrote in his book[68] that Jack Arnett owned a saw mill south of Ardmore, near Piney Grove. In 1897, the governor control broke and the sawmill went out of control killing Jack Arnett, George Cook, and Sim Whitt. Simeon Whitt was the son of Mary Polly Merrell Whitt and John Watson Whitt.

First Train on Old Railroad Bed – "It was…in 1898 that the first train ran on the new railroad down by Taft, Elkwood, Bobo and Capshaw. It would turn back at Capshaw (because) this is as far as the railroad track went. The railroad helped to give some men employment in buying cross-ties. People would get 10 cents to cut and hew the wood ready for the track for each cross tie they finished. My father would hew ties. He would cut and hew house logs, too." [69]

---

[68] "As I Remember it" by Odie Jones, 1979
[69] "As I Remember It" by Odie Jones, 1979

Faces and Places of Yesterday

Jack Whitt – According to Mr. Odie Jones, Jack Whitt was his first teacher. Since Mr. Jones was born in February 1894, that means he would have entered first grade about 1900. Whitt taught Mr. Jones as well as his sister Cordelia and brothers Houston and Wash Jones. (*Editor's note: It appears that Jack Whitt was teaching at the old Cedar Hill School then.*)

An interesting tidbit from Mr. Jones' referenced book is that someone recited the following when Whitt was teaching, "Tobacco is an evil weed, from the devil it did precede. It spoils a wife, it burns her clothes, It makes a chimney of her nose. You will see from four to six girls in the woods breaking sticks in their mouth, they will chew a mop, in the box they will sop; it will almost make a monkey laugh to see the girls spit upon the hearth." Mr. Odie himself says he recited this little ditty when it came his turn: "A monkey was sitting on the end of a rail picking his teeth with the end of his tail. Mulberry leaves and calico sleeves, all teachers are hard to please." Poetry was simple in that day!

Pearl Bobo - purchased land from the Jones family about a mile past Piney Grove Baptist Church and built a house and store there. Time frame for this appears to be in the early 1900s. He also had a sawmill in the area.

Grits Mill – Odie Jones' father, out of necessity, designed a way to make grits out of dried corn long before they were ground at mills and sold in bags. He punched nail holes in a piece of tin and patiently rubbed ears of corn that was not quite dry enough to shell to make regular corn mill. These grits were not as dry as the grits you get today, so they had to be cooked the same day. In fact, most food was cooked and eaten the same day since there were no refrigerators during those turn of the century years.

Elkmont Springs Village – had two stores, a blacksmith shop, a hotel and dance hall. The draw was a mineral spring that flowed at the base of the hill below the village. A wire was run from the hotel down the hill to the spring and a bucket would slide down the hill to the spring to the water spout. When it was filled, someone would wind it back up the hill. Wealthy people traveled to this location during the summer to bath in the water and drink the water from the spring.[70]

---

[70] "As I Remember It" by Odie Jones, 1979

126

1909 Storm northwest of Elkton, TN – More than 100 were killed and many injured when a storm hit Elkton that year. Some people called the storm the Bee Spring storm because it caused so much destruction in that area.

Buddy Mitchell Meets Elvis Presley – 1958 – "What do you know? Elvis Pressley's barracks is just across the street from our Buddy Mitchell at Fort Hood, Texas, and he had a chat with Elvis a week ago, Saturday afternoon. I know all the girls will be chasing Buddy when he gets home for a few days this month, to know if Elvis knows if Cash Point is on the map."[71]

Smith Families – There were three Smith families in the area according to Kenneth Smith who has researched the Smiths in Lincoln County: **James S. Smith, John W. Smith and Edward Smith.** John W. Smith fathered Lemuel, Joel, John Jr., Wilson, Nancy who married Robert Clovis (R. C.) Smith, Polly who married Elijah Smith the son of James S. Smith, Madison, Sally, Phillip Hawkins Smith, and three infant children. Another was James S. Smith who was the father of William, Robert Clovis, Elijah, Andrew Jackson, Malinda and Mary Smith. The third was Edward Smith who lived in the Giles County side of Kelly's Creek. So, if you have a Smith ancestor in and around the Cash Point area, he or she is probably a descendant of one of these Smiths. That isn't to say there couldn't be another Smith line lurking in the area with which this author is not familiar. Source of the names of Smith families are from The Smith Family by Kenneth Smith.

Halbert Family – John William Smith married Frances Halbert, daughter of Joel Halbert who was born in Surry County, NC, as was John William and Frances. According to the Compendium of American Genealogy, page 208[72], "Joel Halbert Sr., married Elizabeth Frances Randolph, in 1740 in Essex County, VA. Elizabeth was the widow of John Armstrong Jones. Elizabeth was the daughter of Richard Randolph and Jane Bolling. Elizabeth was the great-great-great-granddaughter of Princess Pocahontas who married John Rolfe.[73]

[71] Cash Point News, Thursday, April 10, 1958, Mrs. Clyde Franklin, Reporter
[72] The Halbert Family (included in The Smith Family history) by Kenneth Smith
[73] The Halbert Family by Kenneth Smith.

Faces and Places of Yesterday

"Pocahontas has been immortalized in many stories in history, books, and movies. Elizabeth was also the 3rd cousin of President Thomas Jefferson. Elizabeth's grandparents were William Randolph and Mary Isham. William and Mary were Thomas Jefferson's great-grandparents. Joel died after October 28, 1754, which was the last record found of Joel. Joel and Elizabeth were the parents of two sons, Joel Jr., and William Halbert." So descendants of John William Smith can claim kinship to not only Pocahontas but also to Thomas Jefferson whose mother was a Randolph. Interesting connections.

Lemuel Smith family – This family moved to Madison County in 1845 and lived there until moving to Limestone County in 1851. Two possible reasons have been given for their move from Kelly's Creek. There was a disagreement with Debby's brother William Birmingham as to who would administer the estate of Caleb Birmingham. Debbie, Lemuel's wife, was Caleb's daughter. The estate was settled in 1845, and the Lemuel Smith family moved about this time. Son Stephen and his wife, Martha Whitt, stayed in Kelly's Creek and lived in the family house on 120 acres inherited by Debby from her father's estate. Lemuel, himself, was a large landowner in Kelly's Creek where he owned 397 acres, and with Debbie's inheritance of 120 acres, brought their total to 518 acres.

The other possible cause of their move was an altercation involving Lemuel's son, Stephen, 18, and his grandfather John William Smith, along with Neil L. Smith, a local bootlegger, who were charged for being involved in an affray. The men were involved in a fight, probably in Elkton, and were indicted. Whether fighting one another or someone else is not known. Stephen was fined $2.50 and ordered to stay in jail until it was paid. Another reason for the move may have been Stephen's run in with the law in 1849. He had been arrested in Giles County for larceny and sentenced to prison for five years. There is little doubt that Stephen's escapades had a bearing on the family's reputation. At that time, showing one's face in public was difficult when a family member disgraced the family. Also people were sometimes asked to leave the church. Moving to a different area was probably the best solution.[74]

---

[74] The Smith Family by Kenneth Smith

In 1850, Lemuel and Debbie sold the 120 acres of land to Elijah Smith. Lemuel died at his home on May 10, 1854 and is buried in Johnson Cemetery in Limestone County. Debbie remained in Limestone County until her death in 1863. She is buried in Johnson Cemetery as well.

These two incidents should not have reflected on the reputation of the Lemuel Smith family, but it was a close community, and the incident was well known. The Lemuel Smith family was a good family who happened to have one person in its midst who found trouble. They were not the only family who experienced trouble in those days. Fighting, stealing, arguments, drinking, tippling (selling liquor without a license) were fairly common events.

It should be noted that Stephen Smith went on to become a good citizen, father and husband after his prison sentence. He became a stonemason, and when the old stone bridge in Fayetteville was built in 1859, Stephen was hired to work on the project. He settled down and became a farmer, a good husband and father. A youthful mistake did not destroy this man. Stephen also served in the Confederate Army during the Civil War joining the Camargo Guards. The story of an account by Joseph Carrigan, a solider in the 8th TN Infantry, as was Stephen, is recorded in the "The Smith Family History," by Kenneth Smith.

Andrew Riley – son of Samuel Gillespie Riley and Nancy Jane Rawls, was born July 28, 1813. He married Martha Caroline Roper on April 4, 1866, the daughter of Bracken Roper and Rosa Emeline Williams. Martha's father Bracken was beaten to death by a Yankee carpetbagger at the end of the Civil War, Sept. 29, 1866. He was beaten because he refused to tell the carpetbagger where his money was hidden.

Andrew Riley himself was a veteran of the Civil War, enlisting Sept. 1863, at age 17. Andrew and his family moved to Huntsville, AL in 1905, residing on Church Street.

Lewis and Sally Mitchell – This couple lived on a farm at Cash Point near the Alabama state line. Sally's father, David Hamilton, gave her the 186 acres on May 5, 1899 for caring for him for 20 years. Lewis was raised around Dellrose, and had not farmed flat land before. After receiving the farm, Lewis said he prayed about it and decided to give flat land farming a try.[75] The couple lived on the farm until Lewis' death in 1928. Lewis was the son of Clem Marcus Lewis and Evaline Evans.   One cute story about Sally Mitchell, who was very tenderhearted, was a story about Sally telling her grandson not to waste firewood. "Don't waste that wood," Sally told her grandson, one of these days there will be so many people around here there won't be enough wood to go around."

Ardmore High School Girls' Basketball – Ardmore High School opened to students in 1927 with J. T. Blacksher as principal. In 1941, a girls' basketball team was started with Flossie Whitt as coach. Members of the first team were: Marceal Willingham, Doris Neaves, Margaret Hastings, Adora Mims, Marie Smith, Frances McDonald, Margarette Merrell, Gladys Colston, and Martha Dean Lewter.   Unfortunately, the team was short lived because the program was ended in 1946 since it was deemed to be detrimental to the health of the young women players.

Blanche School – Blanche School began sometime before the turn of the century. Mrs. Annie Lee Watson was hired to teach in 1919 and taught at Blanche for 43 years. When she came, the school was in an old-fashioned wood-frame building with 3 classrooms, a music room and had a bell in the belfry to signal the beginning and ending of classes. Before she came, however, there was an academy at Blanche that began in 1875 with J. A. Holland as Principal and Sallie T. Downing as assistant. Sometime between 1875 and 1916, the academy apparently morphed into Blanche School since Mrs. Drucilla Hardin Rossen remembered that her mother attended Blanche School in 1890 where she studied Greek as well as the normal subjects. In 1923, Mrs. Ruth McLemore graduated from Blanche, but it was only a 3-year high school at the time.

In 1926, a new school was built, a nice brick building located on Ardmore Highway. The school was a four-year high school, and teachers and students all thought it was something uptown because of the inside bathrooms and water system. Before the school was built, however, J. P. Gracy, the school principal in 1926 said, "There was nothing on the ground for a new high school. We taught in a church and in an old building there close by until they (built the new building.)." There were just four teachers at the school.

[75] The Smith Family by Kenneth Smith

Faces and Places of Yesterday

The first graduating class was in 1927 and included 13 students. They were Gladys Davidson, Lucy Bell Robertson, Virginia Merrell, Mary Jester, Iona McDaniel, Omah McLemore, Lucille Hall, Ruth Hardin, William Tucker, Charles Blair, Carl Stephens, James Watson and Richard 'Vickers. The next principal of the school was R. C. Shasteen, and he was followed by R. D. best in 1931. At that time, the school had seven high school teachers and 26 were in the graduating class that year. J. Herman Daves was also a principal at Blanche from 1938-1946. During that time, hot lunches were started and the elementary school was built. Unfortunately, the high school was destroyed by fire on January 17, 1947.

A new high school was built on the same spot, and continues to stand to this day but not as a high school. Some of the principals at Blanche were: Lee Earl Mansfield, James Schubert, Raymond Phillips, Grady Duncan, J. G. Stephenson, Roy V. Crabtree, Larry Burke and Stanley Mullins.

Kelly's Creek, - "Our neighborhood, we suppose, was well represented at the Huntsville Fair, a large number of our citizens being in attendance. Spencer Leatherwood, whose horses won some reputation recently at the Pulaski Fair, has them now on exhibit in Huntsville. Mr. Leatherwood delights very much in training trotting horses. He has a mile track on his farm, on which he trains his horses. We infer from what we have heard, that if he is not successful, it will not result in a lack of energy in the business.[76] One promising horse was named Young Nettle Keeman.

Sadly, less than a year later the following appeared in the newspaper on Oct. 17, 1889. "It seems fate oft times chooses the things we most dislike and places them before us, one by one, labeled duty, and it now becomes our sad duty to chronicle the death of our worthy brother, Spencer F. Leatherwood, whom the hand of death removed from our midst August 11, 1889. Therefore, be it resolved, that we, the members of the Pleasant Plains Lodge have through his death lost an honored and beloved member, whose loss we keenly feel and deeply regret. Be it further, resolved, that we as a body tender our sincere sympathies to the bereaved family and point them to the Lamb of God that taketh away the sins of the world. Resolved, that a copy of these resolutions shall appear in the Fayetteville Observer, a paper printed in Fayetteville, Lincoln County, and

[76] Fayetteville Observer, Oct. 13, 1883

a copy be furnished the family. Signed: M. B. Parkinson, J. J. Rawls and C. C. Faulkinberry, committee.

Towry and Leatherwood Wedding – Reported on March 4, 1886, Professor Thomas F. Towry and Miss B. M. Leatherwood were married. He was an educator of several years standing. In 1896 there is a mention of Thomas F. Towry serving as the legislative representative from the area. On Aug. 6, 1903, the Honorable Thomas F. Towry died. Towry served in the legislature twice and was highly respected by those who knew him. He was 46 years old when he passed from "congestion of the brain."

Sim and Hazel Smith were both members of Cash Point Baptist Church until their deaths. Sim Epton Smith was 81 at his death. This couple had four children: Bettye who married a McElroy and lived in Nashville, TN. Anna married Maurice Massey, and lives in Brentwood, TN; Harmon Smith is married to Susan Jones and lives in Spring Hill, TN and Ray Smith lives in Russellville, AL. Ray lost his wife in 2014. Mrs. Hazel Smith was a member of Cash Point Baptist for 75 years.

Blanche Class of 1910-11 – The members of the class of 1910-11 were Fannie O'Neal, Virginia Merrell, Martha Ellen Rainey, Louise Maddox, Mildred Twitty, Marie Reynolds, Mary Hardin, Mary McDaniel, Omah McLemore, Richard Vickers, Iona McDaniel, William Tucker, Lucille Hall, Annie Ruth Hardin, Charles Blair, Lucy Belle Robertson, Bunyan Brock, Doak McDaniel, Laverne Colbert, Sarah Flanagan, James Watson, Gladys Davidson, and Alvie Commons. Professor Carroll was their teacher and Roberta Everly was their music teacher.

Carmargo School – Members of the 8th grade class at in 1939-40 were: Naomi Bates, Voncil Smith, Dora Mae Washburn, Irene Honea, Laurine Brown, Mary Ables, Clay Wallace, Delphia Winsett, Doris Mullins, Lewis Carter, and Horton Mullins. Mr. Russell McAlister was their teacher.

Cash Point - The John S. Ferguson home in Cash Point burned sometime in the late 1930s after Mr. Ferguson died in 1936. That left his widow, Mrs. Janie Ferguson homeless. She lived out the remaining years of her life in Ardmore, dying in 1961 at the home of Fount and Dealie

Merrell in Lincoln County, TN. She lived alone until two years before she died, but had to stay with her daughter because of a broken hip. She was a member of Cash Point Baptist Church.

William Wood Ferguson – William Ferguson was born Dec. 4, 1822 in Chester County, NC to Joseph Ferguson and Ruth Wood. He moved to Lincoln County, TN sometime before 1850 and was listed as a member of the household of Meadow White on the 1850 census. He married Margaret Maben or Maybin sometime after 1850. She was born Jan. 1, 1834, in Chester County, SC and was living with the Pittman family in Lincoln County when the 1850 Census was taken. Margaret died Nov. 29, 1913. She and William were parents to several children, one of which was John S. Ferguson. Their home was near Kelly's Creek.

Pleasant Plains- This was the original name for Blanche, TN in 1850. The name was later changed to Blanche in honor of Blanche Rawls. The name change was necessary as there was already a Pleasant Plains post office in Tennessee. The following letter indicates at least one resident was keen on defending Pleasant Plains' reputation in 1850.

From the Fayettville, TN newspaper[77] this letter appeared: "Dear Sir, - Pleasant Plains, Tenn., was commenced by W. W. Petty about the year 1850, with a dry good house. It made but little advancement in the way of improvement until after the war.[78] Since that time it has been gradually growing into a nice country village and now contains several good business houses, carried on by good clever men of this country's raising.

"The firms are all good. Messrs. J. F. and J. M. Byers, do.; M. F. Hamptom & Co., family groceries. It has two blacksmith shops and one wagon shop, also one cabinet shop. We also have a first rate doctor located here from Giles county. I think we have a good society around this little village as can be found in the state. There is a fine church house finished off here this spring, 30x50 feet. We also have a good school. Our church house has (a) fine bell on it, to notify the people for miles around when to attend worship.

---

[77] Fayetteville Observer June 16, 1871
[78] Reference to the Civil War

"Besides these things, the Free Masons have a lodge here. There is also a good Templars' Lodge held at this place of a large membership of the very cream of the county. Furthermore there is a first rate Sabbath School carried on regularly in the new church.

"Mr. Editor, I see you have many invitations to visit Blanche, and spend a few hours with us. I know, Mr. Editor, we have had a bad name, but I think some of our accusers live in glass houses and had better quit throwing rocks and calling us ugly names. I flatter myself that we have a good neighborhood as any in the country. Our people are sober and industrious; nearly all belongs to the church, Free Masons and Good Templars. So, Mr. Editor, if you can't stay all night, you must call and see us in passing. Signed: Old Dad.

A Post Script was added to the above letter: "I forgot to tell you we have a good tin and saddler shop in our little town. We also have about half a dozen preachers in this neighborhood and one attorney at law."

Blanche Cemetery – Blanche Cemetery's oldest grave is that of Nancy Jane Riley, wife of Samuel Gillespie Riley. She died in March 1852. Census records seem to indicate the land was then owned by Luke Rawls. The early records in the county's obituaries refer to the cemetery as The Rawls Family Graveyard. Luke H. Rawls had purchased the land from the Leatherwood family, but the deed no longer exists. The only information about the land transfer comes from an article in the Fayetteville Observer in May 1894. The first deed citing the name Blanche Cemetery is one recorded on Feb. 20, 1930 where C. M. and Bettie Clardy sold six acres to the trustees of the cemetery. The cemetery is managed by a board of directors of the Blanche Cemetery Association. Hannah Rawls, a former Rawls family slave and later a free Black, is reported to be buried in the cemetery.

Blanche Graduating Class of 1935 included Annie Whitt, Kathleen Mitchell, Evelyn Minor, Evelyn McLemore, Edna Paysinger, Doris Masters, Ray Neely, James Smith, Joe Ed Graham, Harold Henderson, Jesse Harden and Gladys Davidson. Their teacher was Lewis Doster and principal was R. C. Shasteen.

Blanche Basketball Champions 1934 under the guidance of J. P. Gracy, coach, included A. D. Puckett, Harold Henderson, Horace Mullins, Woodrow Stephens, Joe E. Graham, Garland Whitt, James Smith and Buford Rowell.

Blanche School Principals – A. W. Carroll, M. L. Bridges, Craig Beasley, John Baxter, Terrill Twitty, J. P. Gracy, Mell Atchley, R. D. Best, R. C. Shasteen, Lewis Doster, Herman Daves, Lee Earl Mansfield, Raymond Phillips, Charles Sarver, J. G. Stephenson, Larry Burk, Stanley Mullins, Buford Beadle, James Shubert, Grady Duncan, Joe T. McFerrin, Jim Steward, Joel Hastings, Ron Perrin and Ricky Stafford, not in order.

Frank W. Vickers [79]–"Mr. Frank W. Vickers, a prominent citizen and longtime church and community leader of Blanche, succumbed to a heart attack at his home in Blanche, June 13.

"He was born and reared in Blanche being a descendant of a family which settled the community and from early life had been active in the affairs of the community. He was born December 6, 1881, the son of Richard Vickers and Sarah E. Woodard Vickers.

"He was a member of Blanche Methodist Church and remained a steadfast member. He was also a member of the Andrew Jackson Masonic Lodge No. 68 and Woodman of the World, Camp 589 at Cash Point.

"Funeral services were held at the church on June 14 with Rev. R. E. Stevenson officiating. His burial was in Blanche Cemetery.

"Pallbearers were B. P. Maddox, John Thomas Maddox, S. A. Stratton, Howard McDaniel, Billy Askins and Raymond Graham.

"Survivors were: one son, R. B. Vickers of Knoxville; one brother Robert L. Vickers of Blanche; one sister Mrs. A. A. Porter of Lynville and several nieces and nephews."

Your Community Shopper established – Helen Stagner came to Ardmore from Pulaski in 1964 and established the first and only newspaper in town. This publication did not start out as a regular newspaper but more as an advertising medium though it did carry bits and

---

[79] Fayetteville Observer, June 29, 1950

pieces of news. Through the years it began to grow into a viable newspaper keeping the community informed of events, activities and government actions. A family owned publication, Helen, her husband Russell, their sons Tommy and Joe were always involved in the business. Today Joe Stagner and his wife Patti Gates Stagner and son Dylan are the force behind the newspaper with the able assistance of long time employee Patricia Owen Coulter. Helen and Russell are both deceased and are buried in Gatlin Cemetery.

Samuel D. White – He was born in Virginia. The 1850 Limestone County census shows the following: Samuel, 51, a farmer with a value of $40,000; wife, Susan, 38; VA; William L,. 24, AL; Maria E., 18; James Samuel 16; AL; Thomas 14, AL; Robert H., 12; AL; Virginia, 8, AL; Edward F. 3; AL and Jane Word, 27; AL, farmer.

In Limestone County deed book, #4, page 107, Samuel White of Lawrence County, AL is listed as an heir of Absalom White, deceased, in a deed that was made to Absalom Lock of Giles County. The land was in Limestone County.

The Pulaski Citizen on May 13, 1859 reported that William E. Eddins (son in law of Samuel White), as owner would open Elkmont Springs on May 25 for visitors.

Eddins stated that the accommodations and conveniences of this pleasant summer resort could not be excelled at any springs in the Southwest. He claimed the springs were high and very healthy, the atmosphere pure and the scenery beautiful.

Ball rooms and dining rooms had been added, along with a ten-pin bowling alley providing the resort with three alleys total. There was also billiard tables and a bar. These facilities were detached from the hotel. Lewis Bird was the bar-keeper and was known for having an orderly and honorable establishment.

The spring was said to have Chalybeate water which was impregnated naturally with salts and iron. This in turn caused the water to have a strong mineral taste. There was also a post office at the resort, and a daily stagecoach came from Nashville going into Athens and returning.

A survey in June 1859 showed there were 454.25 acres owned by William E. Eddens.[80] The property was bounded on the south side by Elk River and lying in District 1, on the headwaters of Reynolds Creek and Piney River. Property lines of the Arnetts, John Rheas, and the Ezell family. Temples, Wadkins and Stanleys were also mentioned in the survey.

Elmont Springs apparently had some important guests namely, General Nathan Bedford Forrest, who reportedly tried the waters.

A Brief Outline of Ardmore History

Mrs. Elizabeth Hamlett[81] in a presentation at the second anniversary of the Ardmore Branch of First National Bank and during the Bicentennial of America celebration July 2, 1976, presented the following items:

1909 – Railroad engineers determined the shortest route between Nashville and Decatur.

1910 – The decision to build the railroad was made.

1911 – Mrs. Hamlett's father, Alex Austin, bought 200 acres of land and built a 60x30 foot store building where a present day hardware store stood owned by both Mabron Lewter and Thomas Rochelle.

1914 – post office was opened as a 4th class on what is now Main Street.

1915 – A two-story brick high school was built with a study hall and classrooms and stage upstairs.

1915 – First Baptist Sunday School was organized in W. F. Mangum's yard. The church was organized in Garrett Whitt's yard.

1916 – Mrs. D. W. Buchanan, who ran a hotel, organized a Sunday School under a brush arbor. This was the beginning of the Ardmore Methodist church. The two lots it is located on were donated by Mrs. Buchanan and Alex Austin. Later in 1955, A. C. Austin and Mrs. Hamlett gave our shares of this adjoining lot to the church.

1918 – The Bank of Ardmore was built. The first cashier was Tully Brown who remained there until his death. It was one of only three banks in Giles County that survived the depression. Alex Austin was president until his death in 1934.

---

[80] Giles County Survey Book, page 313, June 1859
[81] Your Community Shopper article titled, Remember When.... Undated

1923 – The cornerstone of the Methodist Church was laid even though the building was not complete.

1927 – Ardmore High School received accreditation.

1930 – An elementary school was built on the Tennessee side next to Mrs. Lorene Smith's home.

1933 – The Middle Tennessee Burial Association was organized with Toney Rainey as secretary and treasurer.

1938 – The gymnasium was built on one end of the high school.

1939 - A fire destroyed the first store which was built in 1911.

1940 – Ardmore Cheese Plant was built.

1940 – Ardmore Church of Christ was erected.

1956 – A joint water system was established by the city and town.

1957 – Bank of Ardmore was relocated west of the railroad.

1958 – Ardmore Telephone Company became a dial system.

1962 – Land was leased for a park and ball field.

1963 – First National Bank, Ardmore Branch, opened .

1964 – Ardmore's first newspaper, Your Community Shopper, was established as a free bi-weekly publication. Today it is a regular newspaper with paid circulation. It continues to be published each Wednesday.

1968 – WSLV began broadcasting in Ardmore with complete remote broadcasting facilities.

1982 – Ardmore received cable television service.

Through the years, much has been added in Ardmore in the way of businesses, a modern library, fire departments with trained Firemen and EMTs, a sewer system, a modern city building and storm shelter, purchase of the old Baptist Church for the town hall offices and jail, and much more. It's a growing and thriving community.

Wendell Reed Gatlin[82] 78, of 4314 McClain Lane, Huntsville, Ala., died January 27, 1990 at Huntsville, Hospital. Funeral services were held January 19 at Spry Funeral Home with Rev. W. O. McCain officiating. He was buried in Gatlin Cemetery.

A native of Lincoln County, Tenn., he had lived in Huntsville for 52 years. He was a member of the Baptist Church and a retired employee of the City of Huntsville. He was the son of the late Isaac N. Gatlin and Josie Merrell Gatlin of Ardmore, TN.

---

[82] Obituary in The Shopper, January 1990

He was survived by his wife, Roxie M. Gatlin of Huntsville; stepmother Ruby Bond Gatlin of Ardmore; one son, Joe Reed Gatlin of Huntsville, two grandchildren and one great-granddaughter; a sister Corrine Sullivan of Huntsville, and several nieces and nephews.

Foster Daley[83] 71, of Lacey's Spring, Ala., died Monday, Sept. 18, 1989, at Huntsville Hospital. The funeral was held at Laughlin Funeral Home and burial was in Union Grove Cemetery.

Mr. Daly was retired from the Huntsville Police Dept. after 24 years of service. He was a veteran of World War II, and a member of Union Grove Baptist Church.

Survivors listed were three sons: Toney Daly, Jimmy Daly and Donnie Daly all of Huntsville; one daughter, Lesa Daly of Lacey's Spring; five brothers, Billy Daly and Louie Daly both of Ardmore; Fred Daly Jr. of Huntsville, Robert Daly of Park City, Tenn., and Woodrow Daly of Elkmont; two sisters Hellon Karanza of Hazel Green and Louise Bonds of Valdosta, Ga; and five grandchildren.

Gatlin Cemetery – A letter found in the Bible of Mrs. Alma Merrell Campbell written in 1954 by a relative appeared in the local newspaper in 1990.[84] It began:

"In the early part of 1800, Mr.(Isaac) Gatlin[85] bought the land which was then a farm, and moved his family there as a permanent home. He laid off a portion of that farm to be used for a family burial ground. Upon his death, he was buried there in the family plot.

"His son Isaac Gatlin was heir to the farm and moved there to raise his family. During this time, family members were buried in the same family plot. In 1874, N. G. Gatlin bought the farm from his father, Isaac Jr., and moved his family onto the farm. Meanwhile some of the neighbors had begun to bury some of their families and the cemetery began to grow.

---

[83] Obituary in Huntsville Times Sept. 1989
[84] Your Community Shopper, May 16, 1990, Pg. 11
[85] Refers to Isaac Gatlin Sr. who was born in NC abt 1777

"In 1894, Mr. Gatlin deeded one acre to the community to be used for a public cemetery and the acre was fenced in. In 1899, Mr. Gatlin died and the acre was almost full, so his widow, Syntha Gatlin, gave one more acre.

"The farm was then divided up among the relatives, and Mr. Bennie Gatlin inherited the land on which the cemetery is now located, and sold it so that it could be used for a community cemetery. In 1881 there were only 73 graves in the cemetery."

According to other residents, the citizens of the community donated the money for the purchase of the cemetery land from the Gatlin's and those who donated received plots in which to bury their relatives."

Isaac Thomas Gatlin – was born in 1839 and died in 1883. He was married to Sarah Ann Smith, born 1843 and died 1912. Sarah was the daughter of Robert Clovis Smith and his wife Nancy Smith. I. T. Gatlin served in the Confederate Army in the 44th Infantry, was captured by Union forces and sent to Elmira, NY to a federal prison. Though his father Isaac Gatlin Jr., was totally against him serving in the war, he followed what he felt was right and entered the service, which probably caused considerable friction in the family. Isaac Jr., was said to be a "Union" man.

(See Next page for names)

In the photo on the previous page is Sarah Ann Smith Gatlin, seated, with children Isaac Gatlin, seated; and standing l to r, Frank Gatlin, Berry Gatlin and Nanny Gatlin.

Gatlin Family – Isaac Gatlin Sr., born 1776, was born in Butte County, NC,. His wife's name was Elizabeth, but no maiden name has been determined. It is believed that Isaac is the son of Dempsey Gatlin and Elizabeth Bradley. It appears from family research that the family entered this country when the original immigrant, John Gatlin, left England and migrated to Virginia about 1635. Since the genealogy is not proven completely at this point, it will not be included here. However, the Gatlin family has been firmly entrenched in the area since the early 1800s. Issac Gatlin Jr., was born in 1808, in Wilson County, TN and died in 1888 in Limestone County. According to one family researcher, Wanda Gatlin, both Wilson and Williamson County, TN extended to the Alabama state line. It is known that Isaac Sr. along with his brother Dempsey were privates in the 2nd Regiment Mounted Gunmen from Williamson County, TN. After the war of 1812, the 2nd Regiment disbanded in Fayetteville, TN. Records show that Isaac Gatlin bought 163 acres from Oliver Williams in Lincoln County in 1813, as did his brother, also named Dempsey. It is believed that the Gatlins in the Cash Point area are all related through these early settlers.

Bowlin Child Lost - The quietude of Sabbath evening, the 18th, was broken by the announcement that a child was lost. The little eight year old son of Mr. Jasper Bowlin, who lives two miles south west of Blanche,

slipped away from home, telling someone he was going to a grape tree some distance from home, and when at a neighbor's house near sunset he was directed how to go home, but lost the way. He traveled the road from Roperton to Golightly Springs two or three miles, then turning back took another road in the direction of home, but night came on and he wandered into the woods or barrens, as Mr. Bowlin lives in the edge of them. The neighbors gathered and a search began, they continued nearly all night, but in vain as his tracks could not be seen after he left the road. Search was renewed at day light, when it seemed that the whole community turned out and by sunrise forty or fifty men were in the woods. He was found about 10 o'clock in a field near an old vacant house, known as the Dave Hamilton place. He had slept in the woods. The attention of the family of James Ayers, who lives near the Hamilton place, was attracted by his hollowing. He was bare footed, bare headed and without a coat, and when found was cold, hungry and hoarse. When Mr. Ayers approached him, the little fellow embraced him. He was taken into the house and given some food and a coat and carried home to his anxious mother, grandmother and friends. It was thought by some that he would be frozen as the night was very chilly. It was a pleasure and yet sad to see the tears from his parents and gray headed grandparents, but these were tears of joy. The thanked the neighbors for their search and God for sparing and restoring their child.

Farmers are busy gathering cotton and corn. Corn is making a good yield but cotton is short.

The Arkansas fever has been prevailing here the past few weeks, and as a result several families have gone to that state to make their homes.

Miss Dora Simms and two little nieces returned to their home in Temple, Texas, last week.[86]

Account of Lewis H. Merrell's Service in WWI –[87] "During World War I, on September 21, 1917, I was drafted for service with the army on behalf of my country. I was twenty-three years, eight months and two days of age. I was sent to Camp Gordon, GA to begin my training. From there I went to Camp Sevier, SC for the remainder of my training, assigned to Company D, 105th Engineers, 30th Division (Old Hickory).

"In May 1918, we headed for Montreal, Canada, boarded the Talthybius, and by way of the St. Lawrence River, traveled to the harbor of Halifax, Nova Scotia, to meet a convoy that crossed the Atlantic Ocean to Liverpool, England. From there we crossed England to Cover, then across the channel to Calais, France.

"We hiked from Calais, France, to Ypres, Belgium where we were to see our first active duty in the war. The destruction of Ypres, I'll never forget. The city was as flat as new mown hay, and but one street cleared for movement of troops to the front. In September we were transferred to the Somme front in France to support the 27th Division (a New York Division) breaking the Hindenburg line

"On September 29, 1918, I was hit in the right arm with a shell splinter, and the next day my arm was amputated above my elbow in a

---

[86] The Fayetteville Observer, Oct. 29, 1891 Article by Plow Boy
[87] An account of Lewis H. Merrell's WWI service as written by himself, undated.

field hospital near Paronne, France. In a few days, I was sent to Wilson War Hospital No. 3, Reading, England, and was there until moved to the American Clearing Station at Winchester. There I was annexed to the first convalescence battalion leaving for Liverpool and New York.

"On December 21, 1918, we arrived in New York. Then we were sent to Camp Meritt, New Jersey, where we spent Christmas. After Christmas, I was sent back to Camp Gordon, Georgia and discharged January 25, 1919; and I left for home sweet home in Tennessee.

"My trip to Europe is unforgettable; but the experience of war, I've tried to forget. Peace for the world would be its greatest treasure."

Merrell Family Came from NC[88]- "My great-grandfather, Garrett Merrell, and his brother Ben came from North Carolina to Tennessee about the year 1820. Others came with them, but I've been unable to find truthful information as to who they were. It is not known whether Garrett and Ben entered land together or separately, in Giles and Lincoln County, Tenn; but it is known that Garrett lived in Giles County and Ben lived in Lincoln County. The land they entered must have been five or six square miles from Elk Rover to the **Merrell cemetery** (now known as the **Malone Cemetery** and south from Kelly's Creek to Sinking Creek Valley. Where they settled, the land was covered with several varieties of valuable timber; a hilly section, not too rough for cultivation. The same section would be worth a fortune to its owners.

"It has never been known whether Garrett or Ben was married when they came to Tennessee or married after their arrival. ...Garrett was born in 1798 and died Dec. 22, 1865."

Ben Merrell's Death[89] - "This story, handed down by my great uncles, was told to me several times in life by my father James Franklin Merrell, and his cousin John Smith and others who remembered the story as told by former relatives.

---

[88] The Merrell Family Tree Revised 1964 by Lewis H. Merrell
[89] The Merrell Family Tree Revised 1964 by Lewis H. Merrell

"Ben was too old for service in the Civil War and stayed at home with his family. No one seems to remember his wife's maiden name, but her given name was Elizabeth.[90] I once had a conversation with Mrs. Mary Van Hoozier (she was in the eighties at the time) concerning Ben's family; and she related to me that when she was a small girl, she visited in Ben's home and that Ben's wife Elizabeth was a lovely woman and very much admired by all who knew her. Sometime during the war, Ben had to be away from home one day, and some federal soldiers rode by and stopped long enough to swap horses with Ben. They left an old horse, U.S. branded, in Ben's lot, and went their way. When Ben came home his wife told him what the federals had done. It wasn't good news to Ben, but soldiers had his horse and a good start. They had left a horse for him knowing he'd have a team.

"Sometime later, it was necessary for Ben to be gone again. A squad of federals rode up to Ben's house and stopped long enough to look things over, and noticed the horse in Ben's lot was U.S. branded; they decided the horse had been stolen. With his gun in hand, he walked from the house across the yard to his horse, sprang into the saddle, and left in the direction the federals had gone with his horse. He overtook them three quarters of a mile away at a neighbor's house (now known as the Rogers' place) and called for the man who got the horse.

"Right or wrong, a man walked from inside the house to the door and confessed. Ben raised his gun and shot him down. Wheeling his horse, he started for home; knowing the federals would follow in close pursuit. On his arrival home, he told his wife what he had done. As she pleaded for him to hide quickly; Ben walked through the house and out the back door and down the hill to a tree top on the ground, in which he hid and waited. A light snow was on the ground which should have made it easy for the soldiers to find him, but instead, they failed to notice and ran by Ben in the tree, and he emptied his gun among them, wounding several.

"The soldiers he didn't hit turned around and shot Ben to death. The federals carried Ben's hat to the house and gave it to Ben's wife and said to her, if you want his body go get it. It was shocking news to

[90] Ben married Nancy Elizabeth Hopwood, Oct. 11, 1851, History of the TN Branch of the Merrell Family by M. Broadway, L. Ekis and F. Hand, 1970s

144

Elizabeth, but expected. Nothing is known as to how she got Ben's body to the house but reasonable to suppose neighbors did it for her."

It is believed that Ben was buried in the cemetery along with the other Merrell family members. The cemetery is now known as the Malone Cemetery and is located directly across the road from the old Ben Merrell Home.

After Ben's death, Elizabeth and her children left Tennessee and moved to Jonesboro, Ark. Members of that branch of the Merrell family still live in the Jonesboro area.

A **Story about Garrett Merrell.**[91] "Garrett Merrell was a very large man, said to weigh three hundred pounds or more. In his day, riding horses and walking was their source of transportation. It is known that Garrett rode a small pony most of the time. He and his friends would often leave home for a camping and hunting expedition, and they would make their home in the woods for weeks. They hunted wild turkey, deer and smaller game and used hounds for chasing deer by a stand occupied by a hunter. When the deer came within range, the hunter would shoot it down.

"I've been told that Garrett was very exacting both with his family and slaves. Probably, being a slave owner could account for his manner of no foolishness. I remember my father speaking of a Negro who belonged to Garrett as a slave, and the Negro wished to be away during the Christmas holidays. Garrett gave permission provided the Negro put a back log on the fire that would last until his return. A few days before Christmas the Negro cut a sycamore tree, chopped off a large back log and rolled it into the branch for a good soaking. The day the Negro was to leave on his vacation, he rolled the back log to the house and put it on the fire for Garrett. When the Negro returned, only three fourths of the back log was consumed by the fire and the Negro was safe from a whip lashing. It's my guess, the Negro had to know the log would last until his return or else. Garrett was strong, rough and tough; and it's easy to imagine the humbleness of his slaves when they were near."

George and Adeline Reed Merrell – This family lived in Giles County near Union Hill Church. George was a mechanic, blacksmith and

---

[91] The Merrell Family Tree Revised 1964 by Lewis H. Merrell

farmer. He enjoyed hunting, fishing and beekeeping. At one point, Lewis H. Merrell writes in the Merrell Family Tree, he had 100 stands of bees in his yard which covered three quarters acre of land. Some of his stands were as close to the house as 10 or 12 feet. His grandchildren often tried to temp the bees by walking through the beehives, and occasionally, they were rewarded with painful bee stings, but not often. Both George and Adeline were described as being very loving and kind to their grandchildren. Martha Cynthia Adeline was the daughter of George Reed of Kelly's Creek, and she was remembered for her happy nature and laugh. George was the son of Garrett Merrell. George and his brothers James and John all served in the Civil War in the Confederate Army. John was killed in the war. None of these men owned slaves. Slave ownership must have ended with their father.

James Franklin Merrell – He was a farmer and lived on what is now designated as Merrell Road in Lincoln County near Ardmore. He was a farmer, had a blacksmith shop and also hauled produce to Elkton and brought back to his neighbors, products from the store He loved hunting, fishing and farming. He always had a large orchard and garden, as well as farm animals and crops to care for year around. An enterprising man, he taught his sons useful skills and all were mechanically capable. That seems to have been a trait of most Merrell's, along with their love of hunting and fishing. James Franklin Merrell married Margaret Jane Gatlin daughter of Isaac Thomas and Sarah Ann Smith Gatlin. They lived in Lincoln County from about 1909 until their deaths. Later the farm was owned by their son Pitts Merrell, but Fountain Merrell and Lewis H. Merrell both purchased portions of the farm, built homes there and raised their children. Tim McConnell is the only Merrell descendant that now lives on a portion of that land.

Merrell-Malone Cemetery-[92] Lewis Merrell referred to the cemetery as the Merrell Cemetery in his family history quoted earlier in this book (1964), and said it later became Merrell-Malone. T. L. Ferguson said years before his death that the cemetery was called Merrell-Malone at one point, but the name was changed when the Malone family donated land for the cemetery. Kenneth Smith, a genealogy researcher in Lincoln County and one who has studied the area thoroughly for years, confirms that T. L. Ferguson was probably correct in that the cemetery did carry that

---

[92] The Merrell Family Tree, 1964

name. He also said that he has seen the name on old records and that both Joe Roper and Billy Philpot confirmed for him that it was the name of the cemetery. When Elizabeth Hopwood Merrell's husband, Benjamin Wiseman Merrell, was killed she purchased an acre of land near her home (the home was across the road from the cemetery, and it is believed that land was perhaps part of the Merrell Cemetery, but Merrell's were buried there even earlier than her husband. The earliest grave is that of a Tribble according to cemetery records.

This deed was found by Kenneth Smith in Lincoln County recently: Dated December 19, 1878 - Simeon Whitt and wife to J. E. Malone.

"Whereas we have a fee (sic) simple interest in remainder to take effect and be united with the possession after the death of **Nancy E. Merrell** who has a lifetime interest in two tracts of land in the state of Tennessee, county of Lincoln, District No. 17, containing by estimation in all 135 acres and 152 poles being the same more or less. Bounded by: (boundary descriptions omitted here). H. M. Bledsoe, J. W. Puckett.

"For the consideration of $75 to us in hand, we have bargained and sold and do hereby convey to J. E. Malone the fee simple interest in the remainder of the land and he is to have the use, occupation and control of 20 acres more or less. Boundaries agreed upon by the parties lying in the northwest corner of the 1st tract from on....etc.

"This 19th day of December 1878. Signed Simeon Whitt and W.A. M. Whitt. Witnessed by Jas. C. Scott, T. L. Henderson. Date Feb. 25, 1879. Mrs. E. A. M. Whitt was privately examined apart from her husband and agrees to sell the land. W.A. Franklin, J.P, March 18, 1880. Recorded September 14, 1889 at 4;55 o'clock and registered September 17, 1889."

Nancy Elizabeth Hopwood Merrell was the wife of Benjamin Wiseman Merrell who lived across the road from what is now Malone Cemetery. Benjamin was a brother of Garrett Merrell. A few years after Benjamin died, Nancy E. moved to Arkansas with her family, which is probably why Simeon Whitt, the son of Mary Polly Merrell Whitt, was handling the sale. It is obvious to anyone who reads this deed that the Merrell Cemetery was located on this land purchased by Malone. Merrell's were buried there in the 1840s. This should settle any disagreement about how the cemetery was originally named.

147

Faces and Places of Yesterday

Dr. E. C. Forbes[93] – "February 9, 1908, Dr. E. C. Forbes has removed from Cash Point to Howell for the practice of medicine. We recommend him as a most excellent gentleman worthy of every confidence and he has been successful in the treatment of diseases. He has located in a splendid (missing word), and has shown by his selection of a home that he is man of good sense and discernment."

Sawmill Injury[94] – "Mr. Rufus Smith, who was working at the Currin sawmill near Cash Point was seriously injured Thursday. He fell on the saw, which severed his left arm above the elbow, and otherwise lacerated him. Great sympathy is expressed for Mr. Smith"

Deaths Reported[95] "On the 17th, the death angel entered the home of J. L. and Emma Bishop and took a little infant, their only child. It had not been with them only about two and a half months, but long enough to endear itself to them and make it hard to give up. It had been a sufferer all the days of its short life, but it is a consolation to the parents to know it is now free from pain and suffering. Then on the 26th a little child of Frank Dever of McBurg, who was summering at the home of J. H. McCown, of this place, passed away after months of suffering. The former was buried at Prosperity after a funeral service by Rev. A. J. Ranson. The latter at this place (Blanche) by W.W. Twitty".

Death of John Wesley Mitchell [96]- "The community was saddened by the death of its oldest resident, J. W. Mitchell, 87, Saturday morning. Mr. Mitchell sustained a broken hip In September 1955, after which he was a bed patient. "He is survived by his wife, Mrs. Carrie Smith Mitchell, one daughter, Mrs. Lizzie Freeman of California; 4 sons, Eugene Mitchell, Baugh, Tenn.; Reedie Mitchell, Elkton, Tenn.; John W. Mitchell Jr., and H. A. Mitchell of Pulaski, Tenn.; about 20 grandchildren.

"He was the son of Billy Reed Mitchell, a Confederate Veteran, who lost a leg in the Civil War and Mr. John was the last survivor of a big family of brothers and sisters.

[93] Fayetteville Observer, Feb. 9, 1908
[94] Fayetteville Observer, June 24, 1909
[95] Fayetteville Observer, Aug. 31, 1899
[96] Fayetteville Observer Dec. 12, 1956 from Kenneth Smith's files

"Funeral services were conducted by Bro. Maples at Cash Point Baptist Church, assisted by his pastor, Bro. Halbrooks, at 1:30 p.m. Sunday afternoon, burial at the Malone Cemetery in Lincoln County.

Fox Theater - A. C. Austin, son of Alex Austin, served in the military in WWII and was stationed in the South Pacific for 35 months. When he got out of the Army in 1946, he began working to build the Fox Theater, his dream. "It was the first really tall building here," Dovie Austin was quoted as saying years later. According to Dovie, it was built before the skating rink.

"For a 25 cent ticket, which included a bag of popcorn and a coke, parents could drop off their children on Saturday for the matinee and they could stay until we closed," Dovie said. Adult ticks were 35 cents.

The Austin's originally did all the work themselves, but soon hired Billy Smith and Marlon Broadwater to assist them. The movie theater flourished in Ardmore for many years, but in August 1969, the couple decided to close because they couldn't get a decent movie to show anymore.

The theater remained vacant for a while before the Austin's decided to sell in August 1969. He turned down several offers because the potential buyers wanted to open adult theaters. "He told one man that he would not lease him the theater because if the movies he wanted to show were not good enough to be allowed in Huntsville, they were not good enough in Ardmore," Mrs. Austin said. "The building finally sold to a man from Nashville who said he wanted to open a bowling alley in Ardmore. This man sold the theater to another who leased the building to operate adult films," Dovie said. She said her husband was very upset when that happened.

After the adult theater closed, the building was purchased by Leo Smith who opened an appliance store in the space.

Dovie and A.C. Austin had two children: Anne and Susan. A.C. died in November 1989 the same year he was chosen as Ardmore Optimist Club's Citizen of the Year.[97]

---

[97] Your Community Shopper, March 18, 1992

Faces and Places of Yesterday

Ardmore Cheese Plant [98]- A landmark for more than 50 years, Ardmore Cheese Plant closed its doors on Nov. 1, 1991 for the first time in its history. At the time of the closing, the plant was owned by Leon Sanna, president of National Dairy since 1988. During his ownership, the creamery returned to the basics and was producing cheese as it was done in the 1920s with no short cuts and no hurried productions.

Most people remember the creamery was first owned by Thoran Jones, along with Charles Munn of Horse Cave, KY who were partners in the beginning. Munn later sold his shares to Earnest Henagar, and Jones later bought out the Henagar's who also owned a company in Pulaski. By the late 1940s, Jones was the sole owner. His father, Goodloe Jones was also associated with the company for years.

After Thoran's sudden death in an automobile accident on Oct. 5, 1961, Mrs. Merle Jones, his widow, sold the creamery to her brother James E. Beasley of Athens who operated it for several years.

The creamery was next owned by Avalon Dairies who purchased it in 1976. Finally, Mr. and Mrs. Bob Yancy purchased the company and later sold it to Sanna in 1988.

The company was very successful in its heyday. In 1941 it shipped most of its one million pounds of cheese to Great Britain; but locals also enjoyed the cheese. In the 1950s, the company had 1,700 customers.

They also had a contract with Kraft Foods in the 1950s, and sold aged cheddar cheese in hoops of 25 to 50 pounds. It was not unusual for them to sell 32,000 to 38,000 pounds of cheese in the fifties.

Some of those who worked at the company were Taft Simmons, Boots Bryant (husband of Myra), Joanna Fleming, Fran Magnusson and many others. Until it closed, about 25 people were employed there.

Rainey Funeral Home[99] – Gone from the community today is Rainey Funeral Home. Originally located in Blanche, Rainey Funeral

---

[98] Your Community Shopper, March 18, 1992

[99] Your Community Shopper, March 18, 1992

150

home stood at the intersection of Fort Hampton Road and Highway 53 from 1930 until Don Taylor moved the establishment further out on Highway 53. That establishment has been closed for a number of years as of 2014.

A few may still be living who remember that before the funeral home opened, Toney Rainey had a showroom (caskets, etc.,) upstairs over what was later Boggs Furniture/Magnusson's store on Ardmore Avenue in the building built by Tommy White, according to James Rainey who reluctantly agreed to be interviewed in 1992. James who was retired at that date had been a partner in the business with his father and sister Martha Ellen Hargrove.

After Mr. Toney died, the business continued to operate until November 1982 when it was sold to Don and Betty Taylor from Huntsville. That funeral home no longer exists. The current funeral home is Ardmore Chapel Funeral Home. Mr. and Mrs. Rainey are buried at Blanche Cemetery.

Dellrose, TN[100] was first known as Roosterville. Hog Bruce was the founder and first merchant. It has only been a village since 1867. D. C. Sherrill& Co. ran a business there, and there was a good school in the community. Dr. B. S. Stone was a physician in Dellrose. Taverns were numerous in Giles County, and were situated in all parts of the county without regard to towns. Ephraim Parham, Vance Greer, William Cross, Brice M. Garner and John Kelley obtained tavern license in 1811. Collins Leonard, Jesse Riggs, Cornelius Slater, John D. Spain, John P. McConnell, Elisha Boyles, William Garrett, George Stobah, C. R. Milborn, David Cobb, Joseph Dean, John Parks, William Smith, Walter Kinnard, Enoch Douthat, John H. Zevilly, John Houston, John Parks, Thomas Rountree and William Mitchell were other tavern keepers in the early 1800s. These taverns were also known as ordinaries, houses of entertainment, etc.

W.H. Gibbs Fatal Affray[101]– An unfortunate difficulty occurred at Blanche, in the southwestern part of this county, on Tues., 3rd, in which

---

[100]http://freepages.history.rootsweb.ancestry.com/~pearidger/history/

[101] Lincoln County TN Pioneers by Jane Waller. No date on the file.

W.H. Gibbs lost his life at the hands of W.P. Abernathy. It appears that Gibbs had ill feelings toward Abernathy in regard to a woman, and had

declared if an opportunity presented itself he would kill Abernathy. Tues. evening about 3 o'clock Gibbs was standing in the drug house of Beaty & Coats and Abernathy went in and passed by Gibbs who picked up a weight and threw it at Abernathy striking him on the shoulder; it glanced and made an ugly wound on his cheek. Gibbs followed Abernathy, who is a small man, and caught hold of him; they were separated but Gibbs again got to him when Abernathy drew a pistol and fired three shots in succession. The first passed through Gibbs' upper lip and lodged in his head, the second passed through Dr. Beaty's coat and the third lodged in Gibbs' heart. Gibbs, notwithstanding his wounds, retained his hold on Abernathy and was endeavoring to wrench the pistol from him, when friends interfered and again parted them. The wounded man was forced into a chair and immediately expired. The coroner's jury announced it justifiable homicide.

John Merrell Memorial[102] - John Merrell born abt.1835 in Tenn. John was killed in the Civil War on Sept. 19, 1863 during the first day of the Battle at Chickamauga Georgia – known as one of the bloodiest battles of the Civil War.

John was 28 years old when he died and left behind his wife Margaret Rose Anderson, aka Peggy, and three small children: Mary Elizabeth born March 19, 1855 and married Leroy J. Phillips, Louisa E. Merrell born about 1857 and John Jefferson Merrell born about 1859.

John Merrell served in the war with his bothers George W. Merrell and James S. Merrell, both of whom survived the war. John was the son of Garrett and Olive Thompson Merrell of Giles County, Tn. He and Margaret Rose were married March 8, 1853 in Lincoln County, TN.

Merrell 50th Anniversary[103] – Fountain and Dealie Ferguson Merrell celebrated their 50th wedding anniversary on Aug. 1, 1973 with family and friends present. The children attending were Marie (Howard) Broadway, Marge (James) McConnell, Clay (Audean) Merrell, Thomas

---

[102] Recorded on Find a Grave by Doris and Larry Phillips
[103] 50th Anniversary was Aug. 1, 1973

(Dorothy) Merrell, Loretta (Bob) Ekis, Faye (Bill) Hand, and most of their grandchildren as well. Their other daughter Orlean was deceased in 1948 and was never married.

Giles County Circuit Court 1860s and 1870s - In 1860 N. C. Wisend, for grand larceny, was sent to prison for seven years; in 1865, Samuel Marks, for the same offense, was given ten years; and in 1866 Benjamin Abernathy, Stephen Brown, Jacob Kennedy and Meredith Dabney, for grand larceny, were given terms of imprisonment of three years, one year and seven years, respectively. To 1867 Henry Ars, for stealing a horse, was imprisoned for a term of ten years; Pleasant Beckwith, for murder, in 1868, was sent to prison for one year; and John Lightfoot and George Springer were tried jointly on a charge of larceny and each sent up for three yours; in 1869, Caesar Allen, for larceny, was given one year; James Kelley, for rape, was sent up for fifteen years; and Pleasant Madison, for horse stealing, ten years. In 1870, Sterling Eddins and Harup Mason, for larceny, were each sent to the penitentiary for one year; in 1871, James Montgomery, horse stealing, fifteen years; Lewis Swinnea murder, twenty years; William Allen, larceny, five years; Green Turner, horse stealing, sentenced to be hung; Philip Maples, for administering poison, three years; and Lewis Taylor, larceny, three years. In 1872 Jesse Donaldson, Amanda Abernathy, Virginia Abernathy, Felix White and Richard Collier, for larceny, were given terms of imprisonment ranging from fifteen months to four years, while for murder, Jordan Petty was seat up for fourteen years; Jack McGuire, for stealing a horse, twenty-one years; and George Chapman, for forgery, went up for three years. In 1873, John Adams, Isaac Ballentine, Benjamin McDonald and Sterling Eddins, for larceny, were sent to penitentiary for three, one, four and six years, respectively; Andrew G. Downing and Richard Benson were given fifteen and ten years, respectively, for horse stealing. In 1874, William Jones, George Washington and Calvin Rhoades were sent to penitentiary for five, four and seven years, respectively, and for murder Walker Ingram was sent for twenty years, and John O'Connor ten years for horse stealing.

Giles County Circuit Court – 1820's and 1830's - In 1827, for malicious stabbing, James Z. Maclin was sent to jail for 12 months; for assault and battery, with murderous intent, Sterling Harwell was fined $25 and sent to jail for twenty days. In 1830 Arthur Jarnagar for committing forgery and given 39 lashes on the bare back, sent to jail for a week and made to sit in

Faces and Places of Yesterday

the pillory two hours each morning for 3 consecutive days; Dury Smith, for manslaughter was branded on the brawn of the left thumb with the letter M: and sent to jail for one month. In 1836 James McNune was sent to the penitentiary for 2 years for assault and attempt to commit murder.

Mims Family - Morgan and Brown Mims were businessmen in Ardmore for many years. They owned Mims Frozen Foods, and the Slaughter House on what is now named Slaughter House Road. Their father, Dr. W.S. Mims, was a much loved physician in Ardmore for many years. The Dr. Mims' home stood directly behind the First Methodist Church but has been torn down in recent years. Adora Mims was a member of that family and graduated from school in Ardmore.

Floyd M. Brown[104] - Funeral services for Floyd Brown, 70, bachelor of Ardmore, formerly of Bryson, were held at 2 o'clock Saturday at the Bethany Presbyterian Church of which he was a deacon. Burial took place in the Bethany Cemetery, with Rev. Donald White, pastor of the church, and Rev. E. M. Trammell, pastor of Ardmore Methodist Church, officiating. Mr. Brown died at 11 o'clock Friday morning, January 17, at the home of a sister at Ardmore, after a long illness. Born December 26, 1887, in Giles County, he was the son of the late William A. Brown and Ida Rowe Brown. Mr. Brown is survived by two sisters, Mrs. W. S. Mims and Miss Hattie Mae Brown, both of Ardmore.

Leslie Green Brock[105] - Graveside services for Leslie Green Brock, 67, farmer of Elkmont, Ala., were held at 3:30 o'clock Tuesday afternoon at the Old Scrouge Cemetery in Limestone County, Ala. Mr.
Brock was found dead of a heart attack Monday morning at his home. Mr. Brock is survived by his wife, Mrs. Lena Smith Brock; three sons, Alton Brock, Ardmore, Johnny Brock and Jimmy Brock, Arkansas; two daughters, Mrs. Geraldine McKnight, Ardmore, and Mrs. Mary Smothers, Martin, Tenn.; 22 grandchildren and seven great-grandchildren; four brothers, Herman Brock, Oklahoma, James Brock, Missouri, Milton Brock, California, Bunyan Brock, Limestone County, Ala.; and three sisters, Mrs. Ida King and Mrs. Ada Brown, both of Limestone County, Ala., and Mrs. Etta Holder, Oklahoma.

[104] The Pulaski Citizen, 22 Jan 1958
[105] The Pulaski Citizen 17 Jun 1959

Ola Mae Holt Brock[106] - Funeral services for Mrs. Ola Myrtle Holt Brock, 75, Pulaski resident, were held at 2 o'clock Tuesday afternoon at Pleasant Hill Methodist Church, near Elkton. Rites were conducted by the Rev. Mitchell Sawyer, pastor of the church, and burial took place in the church cemetery. Mrs. Brock died at 8:50 o'clock Sunday night at Giles County Hospital after a long period of declining health. Born April 19, 1881, in the Ardmore section, she was the daughter of the late Lonnie Holt and Jennie Naves Holt, and was a member of the Pleasant Hill Methodist Church. Mrs. Brock is survived by her husband, Clint Brock; two daughters Mrs. William Fogg, Toney, Ala., Mrs. Ralph Balch, Capshaw, Ala., twelve children and twelve great-grandchildren; five half-brothers Jesse Holt, Ardmore, Raymond Holt, Elkmont, Ala., Kelly Holt, Memphis and Hubert Holt of Lucedale, Miss, and Leon Holt, Pulaski.

Zebbie Dee Brock[107] Mr. Brock, 74, retired farmer of Elkton, died at 6:30 o'clock Thursday night, September 4, at his home after an extended illness. Funeral services were held at 2 o'clock Saturday at the Bethel Methodist Church in Limestone County, Ala., of which he was a member. Rites were conducted by the Rev. G. M. Bynum, of Decatur, Ala., and burial took place in Gatlin Cemetery in Limestone County. He was born January17, 1884, in Limestone County. Mr. Brock is survived by his wife, Mrs. Vola Smith Brock; three daughters, Mrs. Harold Blackwell and Mrs. Brooksie Mitchell, both of Limestone County, Ala., and Mrs. Walter Traylor, Smyrna, Ga.; two sons, Milan Brock, Hazel Green, Ala., and Charles Brock, Athens, Ala.; nineteen grandchildren and eight great-grandchildren; two sisters, Mrs. Elzie Franklin, Blanche in Lincoln County, and Mrs. Virgie Mealer, Limestone County, Ala.; and four brothers, Odie Brock, Huntsville, Ala., Tommy Brock, Waxahachie, Texas, Clint Brock, Pulaski, and Fred Brock, Limestone County, Ala.

J. Tully Brown[108] - Mr. Brown, 66, cashier of the Ardmore Bank and a leading Giles County citizen, died unexpectedly of a heart attack Wednesday night about eleven o'clock at his home in Ardmore. Funeral services will be held at two o'clock Friday afternoon at the Ardmore Methodist Church and burial will take place in Maplewood Cemetery in Pulaski. Mr. Brown was born in the Bryson community of Giles County

---

[106] The Pulaski Citizen 29 Aug 1956
[107] The Pulaski Citizen, 10 Sep 1958
[108] The Pulaski Citizen, 28 Nov 1951

and was the son of the late W. A. Brown and Ida Rowe Brown. He had been a cashier of the Ardmore Bank since it was established in 1917 and prior to that he was connected with the Alex Austin mercantile business at Elkton and later at Ardmore. He was active in civic and church affairs of the county, having been a member of the Ardmore Methodist Church and a member of the board of stewards. His wife, Mrs. Nancy Cannon Brown, died October 3, 1950, and their son Lt. David Brown, was killed in action in World War II shortly before his mother's death. Mr. Brown is survived by another son, Lt. Col. Harold R. Brown of Rapid City, Iowa; three sisters, Mrs. W. S. Mims and Miss Hattie Mae Brown, both of Ardmore and Mrs. Joe Mansfield of Blanche; a brother, Floyd Brown of Ardmore; and three grandchildren.

Nancy Cannon Brown [109]- Mrs. Brown, 54, died suddenly late Tuesday afternoon, October 3, 1950, at Vanderbilt Hospital in Nashville following an operation performed earlier in the day. Funeral will be held at 10 o'clock Thursday morning at the Ardmore Methodist Church, conducted by the Rev. S. Laws Park, pastor of the church. Burial will be in Maplewood Cemetery in Pulaski. Born July 9, 1896 and reared in Lynnville community, she was the daughter of the late A. O. Cannon and Nannie West Cannon. She was an active member of the Ardmore United Methodist church and its missionary society. She served as a clerk in the Ardmore Bank in which her husband was cashier. In addition to her Husband, Mrs. Brown is survived by one son, Major Harold Brown, U. S. Army Corps, Rapid City, S. D.; two grandchildren; and six sisters, Mrs. Allen Matthews, Columbia, Mrs. T. H. Briggs, Tulsa, Okla., Mrs. D. H. Weldon, Lavonia, Ga., Mrs. N. H. Matthews and Mrs. A. C. Dorris, both of Old Hickory, and Mrs. John A. Ward, Mexico City, Mex. A son, David Brown, lost his life during World War II.

Sam J. Adams[110]- Funeral services for Sam J. Adams, 79, farmer of Limestone County, Ala., were held at 2 p.m. Sunday at Veto Methodist church. Burial took place in Athens Cemetery. Mr. Adams died Saturday in Athens, Hospital. He was born in Alabama, the son of the late Clay Adams and Nancy J. Rogers Adams and lived at Veto for 28 years. He was a member of the Christian Church. He is survived by his wife, Mrs. Easter Appleton Adams, five daughters, Nancy Cannon, Mrs. Ruth Bai---, both of Athens, Mrs. Russ, Miss Geneva Adams and Mrs. Lillian Gates of Veto,

---

[109] The Pulaski Citizen 4 Oct 1950
[110] Pulaski Citizen 18 Nov 1953

Ala.; two sons, Turner Adams of Ardmore and Rufus Adams of Detroit, MI and fourteen grandchildren.

Carter H. Austin[111]- Carter "Pete" Austin, 54, a leading merchant in Ardmore and a magistrate in Giles County Court, died of a heart ailment at 1 a.m. Monday while seated in a chair in his bedroom at home in Ardmore. His body was discovered by his wife an hour later when she went to his bedside to administer medication prescribed by the physician on a routine basis. He had been ill with heart trouble for several months. Funeral services were held at 1 p.m. Tuesday at Ardmore Methodist church. Burial was in the Ardmore Cemetery (Austin family). A native of Giles County, he was the son of Maggie Rawls Austin and the late Alex C. Austin. He was educated at Massey Military School in Pulaski, the University of Tennessee in Knoxville where he was a member of Phi Gamma Delta Fraternity and was a civic leader and steward in the Methodist Church, president of Ardmore Bank and of the Ardmore Hosiery Mill, a member of the Giles County court for 15 years and a member of the town council. He was president of the Ardmore rotary Club and a veteran of WWI. In addition to his mother, other survivors are his wife, Mrs. Catherine Scott Austin, a son, C. H. Austin, Jr., a sister, Mrs. Cheatham Hamlett, a brother A. C. Austin, Jr., several nieces and nephews.

Mrs. Maggie Rawls Austin[112] - Mrs. Austin, 80, a member of a prominent Ardmore family, was fatally injured shortly before 6 p.m. Friday when she was hit by an automobile in Ardmore. Funeral services were at 2 p.m. Sunday at the Ardmore Methodist Church. Burial was in the Austin family cemetery at Ardmore. Mrs. Austin died at Giles County Hospital when struck by a car driven by William Leo Adcock, 19, also of Ardmore, as she was crossing the road in front of her home according to Deputy Sheriff Collins Wilkes. Wilkes said Adcock told him he was blinded by lights of an approaching car and did not see Mrs. Austin in time to stop. Mrs. Austin's husband, Alex Austin, known as the founder of Ardmore, died in 1933. Daughter of the late John J. and Madeline Bearden Rawls, she was a native of Blanche in Lincoln County and an active member of the Methodist Church. She is survived by a daughter Mrs. J. C. Hamlett, a son, A. C. Austin, four grandchildren and three great-grandchildren.

---

[111] Pulaski Citizen 5 Sep 1951
[112] The Pulaski Citizen 4 Feb 1953

Elkton Residents Die in Accident[113]- Walter Van Bates and
Sherman Smith, Elkton residents, were killed near Columbia, Tenn.,
Monday afternoon about 4 p.m. when the truck they were riding in
overturned after an apparent attempt to avoid passing a stopped school bus.
Funeral services for Mr. Bates were held Wednesday afternoon at 2:30 at
the Church of Christ in Ardmore and burial took place in Elliott Cemetery.
Mr. Bates is survived by his wife, Mrs. Isabel Widner Bates, his parents,
Erskine and Ola Ussery Bates, Elkmont, Ala., two daughters Patricia Ann
and Virginia Gayle Bates; two sons Odie Erskine Bates of Elkton and
Forrest Wayne Bates of Decatur; three brothers Lewis, Willis and Alvin
Bates and one sister, Louise Daly.

Services for Mr. Smith were held Wednesday at Union Hill Baptist
church near Ardmore. Burial was in Gatlin Cemetery. He was a member of
Union Hill Baptist Church and was the son of the late Andrew J. Smith and
Martha Jackson Smith. He is survived by his wife, Mrs. Lora Merrell
Smith, three daughters, Mrs. Clark Leming and Mrs. Adrian Leming, both
of Murfreesboro and Mrs. Lewis Ashton Wood, Shelbyville; a son Merrell
Smith, Ardmore; 3 brothers, Samuel of Huntsville, Grady of Loretto and
A.J. Smith of Ardmore; 3 half-brothers, Earl and Lewis Smith, Dallas
Texas and Ernest Smith of California and a sister Mrs. Burns Anderson
of Nashville, Tenn.

Mrs. Jennie Stevenson Merrell[114] - Funeral services for Mrs. A.
R. Merrell, 89, lifelong resident of the Ardmore community, will be held at
11 a.m. Friday at Union Hill Baptist Church. Burial will be Malone
Cemetery. She died at 9:47 a.m. Thursday, Aug. 30, after a long period of
declining health. Born in Giles County, she was the former Miss Janie
Stevenson, daughter of the late Abner Stevenson and Martha Watson
tevenson, the youngest child of her parents and the last survivor of 15
children. She was the widow of A. R. Merrell who died in 1924. Mrs.
Merrell was a member of Union Hill Baptist Church. She is survived by
one daughter, Mrs. Sherman Smith, Ardmore, with whom she made her
home; one son, Nathan Merrell, former magistrate; five grandchildren and
five grandchildren.

Nathan Merrell[115] -Nathan Merrell, 66, a leading farmer of the
Ardmore area and a magistrate representing the First District in Giles

[113] The Pulaski Citizen 19 Mar 1958
[114] Pulaski Citizen 29 Aug 1956
[115] Pulaski Citizen 14 Dec 1958

County Quarterly Court for the past 12 years died suddenly about midnight Monday in Lincoln County Hospital where he had been a patient for a few days. Funeral services were held at 10 a.m. Wednesday at the Union Hill Baptist Church near Ardmore. Burial was in the Malone Cemetery near Cash Point. He was a native of Giles County, the son of the late Andrew Reed and Minerva J. Stevenson Merrell. He was a member of Union Hill Baptist Church, a Bible class teacher, the treasurer of the Baptist Training Union, director of Giles County Farm Bureau, and a member of the Giles County Board of Education. He was a graduate of the Massey School. His is survived by his wife, Kate George Merrell; a daughter, Mrs. Lester Tomerlin; two grandchildren Janice and Sherry Tomerlin; a sister Mrs. Sherman Smith and several nieces and nephews.

William Pink Merrell,[116] Dr. William Pink Merrell, 81, a retired Dellrose physician were held at 11 a.m. Wednesday, May 21, at Bee Spring Church. Burial took place in the church cemetery. Dr. Merrell died Monday night in Lincoln County Hospital. He was a member of the Baptist Church. He is survived by 3 sons, Jack of Frankewing, Dave of Bunker Hill and Virgil of Kerrville, TX; two daughters Mrs. Grady Storey of Dellrose and Dena Merrell, Bunker Hill; four grandchildren and 3 great-grandchildren. *(Editor's note: this obituary states he was a physician. Another record in Giles County indicated he was a veterinarian.) It is uncertain which record is correct. Helen Currin was related to him I believe he was her grandfather.)*

---

[116] Pulaski Citizen 23 May 1951

Faces and Places of Yesterday

A recent photo of Blanche High School (photo courtesy of Bill Hand)

Merrell Family, front left to right, Marge, Marie, Loretta, Faye and Clay,
Back, Thomas, Dealie and Fountain Merrell 1950s

James F. Merrell's Children, kneeling, Pitts and Herman Merrell,
Standing, L to R, Charlie, Francis, Lewis, Odell, Fount and Alma.
(photo courtesy Faye M. Hand).

Faces and Places of Yesterday

Merrell Brothers – L to R – Charlie, Fountain, Herman, Lewis and Pitts Merrell sons of Margaret and James F. Merrell
(Photo courtesy of Faye M. Hand)

(Author's note: It is interesting how the families always were fully dressed in even candid photographs. Times changed a lot after they grew up, and people are now very casual. Seldom do you see anyone in suits and ties unless it is at church, a wedding or some other special event. But even in the 1930s, men and women dressed even when they were visiting parents.)

The James McConnell Family
From left, Tim McConnell, Jerry McConnell, Mark McConnell, James, Beverly McConnell and Tony McConnell.

Dorothy Watkins Merrell wife of Thomas Merrell

**James and Marge McConnell with children Tony,
Jerry and Beverly**

**Eris Merrell Tomerlin Smith and
Lucille Campbell Bailes**

Peggy and Calvin Holt

Giles County Tavern, Ardmore, TN

Faces and Places of Yesterday

Merrell Cousins at Reunion in 2007
Left to Right, Fred Stevenson, Sarah Finley, Doris Secrest, Annis Godwin,
Willard Campbell in back, Faye Hand, Elden Merrell and Terrell Merrell

Kathy Holman, now deceased, shown here
with twin grandsons Daniel and David Lawhorn.

166

Ardmore's Main Street[117]

George Biles husband of Trudy Hamilton Biles moved to Texas

Blanche TN first school
where Virgie Lewter went to school.

First Blanche School - Where Virgie Lewter later Holt went to school – note the bell tower.

1906 Singing School at Cash Point Baptist Church

Bales of cotton –Sarah Mitchell and Ruth Mitchell

Lewis Merrell and Mary Merrell about 1922
Note the prosthesis on the right hand of Lewis – a result of his WWI
service in Europe.

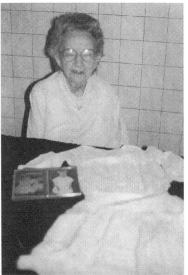

Ruby Gatlin Barnett with dress she wore
as a child

John B. Mitchell holding Vergie, Minnie holding Pitts and Elsie standing (Photo Courtesy of Kenneth Smith)

Skyway Café in Ardmore, TN Selena Owen and Bus Smith are in this photo.
(photo courtesy Patricia Owen Coulter)

Modena Foster Smith
Ardmore Telephone Operator 1950s

172

Dealie Ferguson Merrell with Loretta Merrell
about 1942 in Louisville, KY

George Washington Merrell

David Roper in front of sign at Roper Grocery
In Cash Point

174

Henry and Calline Lewter with son Dewey. They were the first charter members of Union Hill Baptist Church [118]

The Sherman & Lora Smith Family - Children Jeneal, Lucille, Martha Drew and Sherman Merrell Smith

[118] Photos on this page provided by Laurene Schrimsher

Clara and Clint Van Hoozer and Ida and Ed Toone[119]

A.B. and Alice Bond

---

[119] Photos on this page provided by Laurene Schrimsher

Kate Merrell and grandchildren, Janice and Sherry Tomerlin[120]

The Lackey Family – Union Hill

---

[120] Photos on this page provided by Laurene Schrimsher

Sam and Bessie South McConnell
They lived on Bayless Road in the 1940's-50 and in Ardmore afterward. (Photo courtesy of Robbie Hayes)

Paul McConnell
(Photo Courtesy Robbie Hayes)

The Sam McConnell Family

The Children of Sam and Bessie South McConnell celebrated the couple's 50th anniversary at Piney Grove Baptist Church July 1975: L to R, front, row Betty McCown, Faye Eakes, Linda Faulk, Robbie Hayes (behind Linda), Mrs. Bessie McConnell, Mr. Sam McConnell, Willa Dean Blankenship, Carrie McConnell and Mary Dean Lewter; back row, Glen, Ray, Paul, James, Woodrow, Larry and Walter (Moe) McConnell.

**Janie Hamilton Ferguson daughter of Henry Clay Hamilton
And Amanda Bonner Hamilton**

**Elizabeth Hamilton Vickers daughter of Herny
Clay Hamilton and Amanda Bonner Hamilton**

180

Hamilton and Ferguson Family

L to R, front, James David (Jim) Hamilton holding unknown infant, George Washington (Bitts) Hamilton with unknown female, John Sherrell Ferguson holding daughter Geneva, back row, Ethel Ferguson Hamilton, Martha Hodges Hamilton, Sarah Jane Hamilton Ferguson and daughter Dealie B. Ferguson. The children each are holding are probably their own since the wives are in back of their husbands.

181

Faces and Places of Yesterday

Mystery Photo

This photo came from Tom Walker of Bastrop, Texas. It was shown to both Houston Franklin and Houston Wright before 1993 and both men believe this is the old Hopwood Place on State Line Road. It may be a picture of Hopwoods or Walkers who lived in the area. If anyone can ID, please contact the author. As you can see it is an old dog-trot type log house.

Faces and Places of Yesterday

30th class Reunion of the BHS Class of 1956 made in 1986.
It is included here because several of this class are now deceased. Members, front, l to r, Adalyn Whitt Stroud, Lynn McMillin Towry, Martha Jones Stone, Peggy Lewter Hopkins, Aline Holt Hargrove, 2nd row, Loretta Merrell Ekis, Martha Ann Mitchell Walker, Doris Massey Wallace, Elaine Holman Green, Ellen Faye Monks Brooks, Wanda Holt Owens, Peggy Edwards Vickers; 3rd row, John Lee Monks, J. W. Fleming, Aaron Lewter, Charles Wallace, Arzell Hall, Danny Magnusson, 4th row, Ronnie McBride, Fred Benson, Jimmy Green, Lanier Gray and Rabon Colbert.

Dr. John W. Maddox
Ardmore Physician

Dr. T. C. Berry
Ardmore Veterinarian

Sally Hamilton Mitchell at age 90

Emaline Roper
(Photos on this page courtesy of Kenneth Smith)

The Berry Family – Dew Malone Berry, Doctor T. C. Berry, DVM,
And Son, Bill Berry, during the Giles County Sesquicentennial.
Bill Berry, DVM, now owns and operates Berry Animal Clinic off
Highway 53 - Ardmore. (Photo Courtesy of Dr. Bill Berry)

Afterward

As I worked my way through all these photos, trying to get a good cross section of the older generation who peopled the area, I kept thinking about so many of whom I did not have photos and wished I had. I feel remiss in not getting more, but I knew that space was limited at best. I do apologize for not having photos of numerous business people from Ardmore who owned places in the early 1900s, but I did not know exactly whom to contact. In copying old items from newspapers, etc., I've tried to leave much of the style in which it was written because that is another piece of history.

I hope that you have enjoyed this effort. It has been a labor of love. If I've missed giving credit where credit is due, please accept my sincerely apology.

If you like the book, please go to www.amazon.com and review the book. You may also contact me at Ekis.al@gmail.com or call me at 913-851-3784. If you are unable to order via the internet, this book may be purchased by going to any book store and using the ISBN number to order.

Loretta Merrell Ekis

Faces and Places of Yesterday

As you travel around
Take a look at the old houses and
Barns falling into disrepair...
A by-product of the modern age.
They are no longer needed and used.
What was once an open door welcoming
Friends and family, now hangs
Loosely by one hinge.
Logs from old cabins
Either rot or are removed for other
Uses, leaving only stone supports as
Evidence of where a family once lived, loved and
Gave birth to another generation.
When you notice these relics of
The past, remember that
Nothing is permanent in this world.
From dust we are made and to
Dust we will return-- happy in
The knowledge that the spirit shall
Live on in eternity and in the hearts
Of those left to view old
Photographs of another time.
LME

Quotes from my readers

"I have just finished reading your wonderful book about Captain Benjamin Merrell. I love your style of writing and your command of the "kings English." I, too, am a direct descendant of Captain Merrell and knew a bit about his life. However, there were several facts that I was not aware of. For instance, I did not know Jemima's line." P.M. Jones, NC after reading *"The Blood of Patriots – the Story of Captain Benjamin Merrell – American Patriot."*

"Even though I'm not a descendant of the Captain Benjamin Merrell family line, I am a genealogist interested in the various Merrill and Merrell families who came to America. I would think that anyone born into a Merrill or Merrell family in the United States would know at least a little about this great American hero, but I was also very pleased to see the wonderful job Loretta did elucidating the life, times and hardships of all such colonial families regardless of surname." D. Merrell, Texas after reading *"The Blood of Patriots."*

"Loretta really hit the 1950's life in the south. Being a northern girl, myself, I enjoyed reading to both compare and contrast. We are from the same age group. Very humorous, but also very accurate from what my southern friends say. I have loaned the book already!" M. Ragusa, CA, after reading *"Southern Ways and Southern Days."*

"Thanks to Loretta for a super writing of "Southern Ways and Southern Days". Loretta says in her book that you can't go home again, but I disagree. Reading her book took me on a wonderful trip into my early life in Tennessee and Alabama." J. Myers, FL after reading *"Southern Ways and Southern Days."*

Notes

Notes

Faces and Places of Yesterday

Made in the USA
Middletown, DE
22 November 2017